The End of
American
World Order

The End of
American
World Order

—— Amitav Acharya ——

polity

First published in 2014 by Polity Press
Reprinted 2014, 2015 (four times), 2017, 2018

Polity Press
65 Bridge Street
Cambridge CB2 1UR, UK

Polity Press
350 Main Street
Malden, MA 02148, USA

ISBN-13: 978-0-7456-7247-2
ISBN-13: 978-0-7456-7248-9(pb)

A catalogue record for this book is available from the British Library.

Typeset in 11 on 13 pt Sabon
by Toppan Best-set Premedia Limited
Printed and bound in the USA by LSC Communications

The publisher has used its best endeavours to ensure that the URLs for external websites referred to in this book are correct and active at the time of going to press. However, the publisher has no responsibility for the websites and can make no guarantee that a site will remain live or that the content is or will remain appropriate.

Every effort has been made to trace all copyright holders, but if any have been inadvertently overlooked the publisher will be pleased to include any necessary credits in any subsequent reprint or edition.

For further information on Polity, visit our website: www.politybooks.com

Contents

Tables

Abbreviations

ANC	African National Congress
ANZUS	Australia, New Zealand, United States Security Treaty
APEC	Asia-Pacific Economic Cooperation
ARF	ASEAN Regional Forum
ASEAN	Association of Southeast Asian Nations
ASEM	Asia-Europe Meeting
AU	African Union
BASIC	BRIC plus South Africa, minus Russia
BRIC	Brazil, Russia, India, China
BRICS	Brazil, Russia, India, China, South Africa
BRICS AM	BRIC plus South African and Mexico
CENTO	Central Treaty Organization
CIVETS	Colombia, Indonesia, Vietnam, Egypt, Turkey, South Africa
CSBM	Confidence and Security-Building Measures
CSCE	Commission on Security and Cooperation in Europe
CSSDCA	Conference on Security, Stability Development and Cooperation in Africa
G7	Group of Seven
G8	Group of Eight
G20	Group of Twenty
GATT	General Agreement on Tariffs and Trade
GDP	Gross Domestic Product
GNI	Gross National Income
EAEC	East Asia Economic Caucus
EAEG	East Asian Economic Group
EAS	East Asia Summit

ECOWAS	Economic Community of West African States
EEC	European Economic Community
EU	European Union
EUISS	European Union Institute for Security Studies
FEALAC	Forum for East Asia-Latin America Cooperation
GCC	Gulf Cooperation Council
HST	Hegemonic Stability Theory
IBSA	India, Brazil, South Africa
ICC	International Criminal Court
ICISS	International Commission on Intervention and State Sovereignty
IMF	International Monetary Fund
MERCOSUR	Southern Common Market
MIST	Mexico, Indonesia, South Korea, Turkey
NAFTA	North American Free Trade Agreement
NATO	North Atlantic Treaty Organization
NEPAD	New Partnership for Africa's Development
NGO	Non-Government Organization
NIC	National Intelligence Council
NIEO	New International Economic Order
OAS	Organization of American States
OAU	Organization of African Unity
OECD	Organisation for Economic Cooperation and Development
PPP	Purchasing Power Parity
R2P	Responsibility to Protect
RTA	Regional Trade Agreement
SAARC	South Asian Association for Regional Cooperation
SADC	Southern African Development Community
SARS	Severe Acute Respiratory Syndrome
SCO	Shanghai Cooperation Organisation
SEATO	Southeast Asian Treaty Organization
UK	United Kingdom
UN	United Nations
UNSC	United Nations Security Council
US	United States
USSR	Union of Soviet Socialist Republics
WTO	World Trade Organization
ZOFPAN	Zone of Peace, Freedom and Neutrality

Acknowledgments

An entire first draft of this book was completed while I was a Christensen Fellow at St Catherine's College, Oxford, during the Trinity term of 2013. I am grateful to the fellows of the College, especially my academic host Louise Fawcett, for electing me to this prestigious fellowship and making my stay with them highly enjoyable and intellectually rewarding. Andrew Hurrell and Yuen Foong Khong indulged me by critically discussing and reacting to some of the themes of the book.

A lecture at Oxford's Department of Politics and International Relations on June 6, 2013, moderated by Duncan Snidal, allowed me to have the ideas and arguments of the book debated among a lively audience of faculty, students, and visitors, and brought closure to the book.

The encouragement of Louise Knight of Polity Press is what got me to write this book in the first place. Discussions with my students in the course of my graduate seminar on "New Multilateralism" at American University, Washington, DC, during the Fall of 2012 helped shape and sharpen the book's arguments. I thank Louis Goodman for his constant encouragement and for reading and commenting on the entire manuscript, as well as Allan Layug, my faculty assistant at American University, and copy-editor Helen Gray and production editor India Darsley for editorial assistance and management.

Summaries or parts of the key arguments of this book were presented at Rhodes University in South Africa on March 7, 2013; the University of Cape Town on March 11, 2013; the Transworld Conference at Chatham House, London, on April 26, 2013; Meiji University, Japan, on July 1, 2013; and the Conference on "Rising Powers and Contested Orders in the Multipolar System" in Rio de Janeiro on September 19–20, 2013. I thank the organizers of these events for helping to generate valuable feedback (and controversy) on my arguments.

– 1 –

A Multiplex World

Pundits and policymakers have described the emerging world in a variety of ways: "multipolar," "polycentric," "non-polar," "neo-polar," "apolar," "post-American," "G-zero," and "no one's world."[1] At the heart of these phrases are differing and often uncertain beliefs about America's position and role in world affairs. Some of them address the issue of America's "decline," which remains a matter of intense and inconclusive debate. Many Americans and some outsiders vigorously contest the "decline thesis." Among those who accept it, sometimes with a dose of reluctance, are those who optimistically argue that the order established by the United States has been so widely accepted, deeply rooted and legitimate that it will continue to define the twenty-first-century world and might even co-opt its potential challengers. They also warn of the dangers that await the collapse of that order, including multipolar rivalry, regional fragmentation, and other evils.

This is not a book about the decline of the US, but the decline of the American World Order. The issue of America's decline, which I discuss briefly in chapter 2, and the fate of the American World Order are not one and the same, although they are often conflated in public debates. The American World Order is coming to an end whether or not America itself is declining.

A word about the term "American World Order" here. I use this term almost interchangeably with "American-led liberal hegemonic order,"[2] a claim about the sweeping and as-yet-unfinished US hegemony in world politics. American World Order (which I shall also use in its abbreviated form AWO) is perhaps more faithful to what is presented as a product not so much of American *hegemony* as of *American* hegemony,[3] and whose scope and impact is supposed to have a universal quality. Moreover, my understanding of the term is partly based on John King Fairbank's notion of the "Chinese World Order." For Fairbank, the Chinese World Order was a benign hegemony centered on and dominated by China until destroyed by the Western powers.[4] It was built around "a sense of superiority and hierarchy without the concepts of sovereignty, territorially-bounded nation states, or a balance of power. Rather, it was given order and unity by the universal presence of the Son of Heaven."[5] But there are important differences between the old Chinese order and the American World Order of the post-World War II period. The Chinese World Order was a suzerain system; hence Fairbank used the term "world order," rather than "international order." The AWO is built around a world of territorially bounded nation-states, although its respect for state sovereignty can be overstated.[6] And despite differences, the "abiding sense of superiority and hierarchy" is a shared feature of both, as is the idea that the system was "given order and unity by the universal presence" of the leading power. More important, just as the concept of a Chinese World Order is built around a narrative of peacefulness and benevolence about the benefits of trade and protection accruing to its followers (the emperor gave more gifts than he received from those bearing tribute), the AWO narrative also relies heavily on hegemonic benevolence providing global public goods such as trade, security, and multilateral cooperation and the hegemon's sacrifices from incurring trade imbalances to shedding blood for foreigners.[7] And just as the Chinese World Order was not really a global order, but comprised a group of states around China mainly in East Asia, the American World Order was for the most part not really a global order. Rather, it was a relationship among a group of like-minded states, mostly Western, led by the US. A sense of conflation between the liberal hegemonic order and world order more generally is one of the problems with the claims of the former, as argued in chapter 3. And neither order was as benevolent as its supporters have presented it to be.[8]

It is the end of this sort of a conception of American World Order that I examine in this essay. What comes in its place is as yet uncertain. Few can deny that America will continue to play a central role in world affairs for the foreseeable future. But the idea that the hitherto "American-led liberal-hegemonic order" or American World Order will persist, even in a "reconstituted" form, is questionable. This is because a key problem in debating the persistence of the American World Order or the American-led liberal-hegemonic order is that we can genuinely disagree about *what might persist*, and *what its form might be*. Myths about the old order abound. Was there really an American-led liberal hegemonic order in the way it has been presented to us? If it ever existed, what were its membership, scope, and benefits? Some of the claims about what that order actually represented, how far it extended, and the benefits it produced, while not unfounded, are selective and exaggerated. The scope of that order has been more limited, and its contribution less consistently benign to those outside of it than its proponents suggest. This is an issue I take up in chapter 3.

And while these questions about the past of the American World Order remain unsettled, we have further problems in discussing the future of that order. What might its reconstituted form be if it persists into the future? Ideas about the nature and extent of its reconstitution are not specific enough to serve as a credible point of reference. This is no easy task, but demands serious reflection and debate.

This, then, begs the question: how much change is involved in this reconstruction, without that order losing its essential characteristics, the most important being that it was *American*-led or dominated? The challenge here is our lack of a clear picture of an altered or reconstituted American liberal hegemony. How much change and accommodation does it need to make to ensure its survival? Too much might lead to the loss of its essential features and modus operandi. Too little means a reduction in the kind of legitimacy that would both reinvigorate and enable its effective functioning within the new realities of world politics. At the same time, the potential of the American World Order to shape multilateralism after its own image and interests and to co-opt the emerging powers is overrated. Any reconstituted American hegemony has to change a lot, and accommodate, rather than co-opt, other forces and drivers, including the emerging powers and regional groups. It has to adapt to a new multilateralism that is less beholden to American power and purpose.

By "the end of American World Order" then, I refer not just to the end of the "unipolar moment," as discussed in chapter 2, but also of the more long-term physical and normative force of American hegemony that might drown out other approaches, either globally or regionally. Such a notion of liberal hegemony was somewhat mythical to start with, and is unlikely to define our future. The age of global dominance by any single power as the world has previously experienced under Britain, then America, is over.

This does not mean that the "emerging powers" can singly or collectively step into the breach as the American World Order ends. To be sure, their role is critical to defining the future of world order. But if the idea of a liberal hegemonic order is based on an exaggerated projection of the "shadow of the West," a good deal of discussion of the role of the emerging powers is based on what might be called the "hype of the rest." To a large extent, their role lies in preventing or frustrating the continuation of American World Order rather than providing an alternative form of global governance on their own initiative. The lack of unity, vision, and resources makes an alternative construction of global order by the emerging powers unlikely. Hence, cooperation between the established and the emerging powers is critical to the future of global governance. The emerging powers by themselves neither represent nor exhaust the possibility of an alternative, or post-hegemonic, global governance structure. Moreover, while the liberal hegemonic order narrative tends to downplay regional forces or present them as a threat, the emerging power hype ignores the fact that securing regional legitimacy is a major prerequisite for their global ambitions. The central theme of chapter 4 concerns the limits of the role of emerging powers in global governance.

The narrative underpinning the American World Order paints an unduly alarmist picture of the consequences of its decline. Most American commentators do not think its decline would be a good thing for anyone. Even those who do not dispute the signs of decline and accept it as a fact of life hope that the consequences would not be catastrophic for America itself and the world. In this view, the end of the American World Order could result in acute multipolar rivalry and fragmentation of the world into competing regional blocs, as happened in Europe in the nineteenth and early twentieth centuries. I dispute this alarmist view. While no one can predict the future, there are reasons to believe that the decline of the American World Order might even be good – both for America itself and for the rest of the world.

The liberal hegemony narrative not only assumes that the emerging powers could be co-opted into the American World Order. It also regards some other foundations of global peace and stability, such as regionalism, in a negative light. Many liberal internationalists have generally been distrustful of regional orders. The United States has been quite selective or indifferent in its support for regionalism around the world. These fears may be exaggerated because the nature and role of regions and regionalism have changed considerably since World War II. As discussed in chapter 5, regionalism is less polarizing, and more open today than ever before. Thanks to inter-regionalism, the rise of alternative non-European forms of regionalism, and the proliferation of transnational issues that regional groups must contend with, regionalism has become more open, inclusive, and multidimensional. While regionalism alone is not a sufficient basis for constructing global order, it cannot be ignored in any meaningful discussion of the future of world politics and deserves serious attention in any discussion of what might take the place of the American World Order.

How are we to visualize this decentered, complex, multidimensional world? Joseph Nye likens the current structure of world politics to a "complex three dimensional chess game." The chessboard has three layers. The top layer represents military power, which is largely unipolar and likely to remain so for some time. The middle layer is economic power, which has already become multipolar. The bottom layer consists of transnational or cross-border transactions in which non-state actors, ranging from global social movements to terrorist groups, operate largely outside of government control.[9] In this bottom layer, "power is chaotically dispersed."[10]

But Nye's metaphor, as might be expected from a game of chess, is mostly about power and its mechanics. Ironically, it does not even account for his much-vaunted notion of "soft power." (Do you use persuasion in a game of chess?) A better metaphor for visualizing world order, while looking beyond the language of hegemony or polarity, is that of a multiplex cinema[11] – multiplex being "a complex that houses several movie theaters."[12] There may be one film running in different theaters in the same complex, but more often there are different films in different theaters in the complex. In a multiplex world, we have different producers and actors staging their own shows concurrently.

In a multiplex, the audience can watch different types of movies. Some might be thrillers and Westerns, with violence, crime, ruggedness, and heroism as prominent themes, like the Hollywood type. Others could have passion, tragedy, song, and dance, like the standard Bollywood fare. We would have Kung-fu films produced in Hong Kong and Taiwan, and Chinese patriotic and propaganda films made in the mainland since the communist revolution. Some would be social dramas, like the increasingly popular Korean exports. There would be plenty of scope for "indy" films alongside those from established houses like the Universal Studios or Columbia Pictures. The multiplex often has one or two theaters that are much larger than the others. It can hold the blockbuster films alongside a variety of independent films. Every now and then, one of those small films might grow in popularity, attract larger audiences, and move to a bigger theater. No single director or producer would monopolize the audience's attention or loyalty. To be sure, some would be mega hits and others spectacular flops. The audience has a choice of shows. They can also watch, enjoy, and compare several or all of them.

Our world is shifting and to some degree has already moved into a version of the multiplex cinema. The liberal hegemony story as presented to us by its leading American proponents is the equivalent of one movie at a time in one theater. After the run of the British, the American movie has been showing for a while. That movie (perhaps a Western, à la John Wayne) was scripted, produced, and directed by the US, with itself as the lead actor. In the multiplex world, the American show is joined by a variety of others with different plots, producers, directors, and actors. In a multiplex world, the making and management of order is more diversified and decentralized, with the involvement of established and emerging powers, states, global and regional bodies, and transnational non-state actors. The latter include good global civil-society groups and norm entrepreneurs, and villains such as al-Qaeda, drug lords, people smugglers, and greedy corporations (although corporations can go either way).

In a multiplex world, there are hits, but also flops, like some of the emerging powers currently so hyped fading away because of the middle-income trap, domestic instability, or the hangover from regional conflict. (India, China, Brazil, South Africa, and Russia each has such a potential.) Although the American show may continue to dominate the box office for a while, the audience may lose interest when faced with more choices. Leadership is plural and is conducted in different styles and modes, just as a multiplex runs movies of different varieties. Yet being under one complex means sharing a common architecture and being in an interdependent relationship. And the security screening at the entrance to the entire complex implies that collective and common security mechanisms are at play.

American power would be an important part of a multiplex world. But rather than the mythical Leviathan, it is more likely to be the large but vulnerable (and occasionally errant) mammoth of the Ice Age – or even its genetic cousin, the elephant. A multiplex world would be a world of diversity and complexity, a decentered architecture of order management, featuring old and new powers, with a greater role for regional governance.

The future of world order thus lies not in a restored American hegemony. It does not rest on any or all of the emerging powers acting on their own or in concert with the established powers. A regionalized system of security and economic cooperation alone will not fulfill the requirements of world order either. All of these elements, including a constrained but still significant US power, are likely to exist to varying degrees and shape the future world order. Against this backdrop, chapter 6 examines the possible middle ground between a concert among the established and emerging powers and a network of predominantly regionalized orders. That middle ground may well give definition and shape to a multiplex world. The difference between a multipolar world and the multiplex idea is twofold. The former, at least in its traditional sense, refers primarily to the existence of several great powers in an international system and the distribution of material capabilities among them. It does not necessarily define the quality of their relationship, which therefore becomes a matter of debate (e.g., whether multipolarity is more stable than bipolarity, as will be discussed in chapter 2). Multiplex stresses not the number of powers but the interdependence among them. Second, a multiplex world is more decentered than a multipolar world, with greater scope for local and regional approaches. It limits the possibility of a collective hegemony of the great powers over the rest, which is quite possible in a multipolar world. A multiplex world allows the audience more variety, more choices, and more control over what they wish to see. In this respect, a multiplex world is more of a two-way construction. The producers are more sensitive to the demand-side, or the changing audience tastes while developing their scripts, even as they try to shape and influence the audience with new ideas and trends (albeit offering them in greater variety). Overall, the agency in building world order is more dispersed, and lies more with the audience than with the producers (great powers).

Moreover, the films showing in this multiplex are four-dimensional. The three-dimensional concept measures length, height, and depth. In a multiplex world, these correspond to power, geographic scope, and leadership, but the fourth dimension, time, is also of critical importance. A four-dimensional perspective generates a more accurate picture of our past and future world order than the singular and domineering perspective of the liberal hegemony idea. From this perspective:

Height represents the distribution of power, defined in terms of the traditional notion of hard power, which forms the basis of an international hierarchy and ordering of nations. It is the world of great powers in the classical sense. I do not believe that traditional power politics would disappear from the multiplex world, but shifts in the distribution of power, including the relative decline of the US (chapter 2), the rise of Asian nations such as China, India, and Brazil, would reshape the management of world order. These rising powers will be strong enough to thwart a return to unipolarity under the US, but not powerful enough to dominate the world on their own terms. (chapter 4)

Length is the extent and dispersion of order; it captures regional orders on a global scale. Unlike the liberal order during the cold war, whose purview did not include such big nations as the USSR, China, and India (chapter 3), or the cold war bipolar order which was centered on the "central strategic balance" and Europe, and viewed third world regional conflicts as permissible, and third world regional orders as insignificant, the multiplex conception would be global in scope, multi-regional, but with interdependence and institutions within and between regions. (chapter 5)

Depth refers to the quality, robustness, and legitimacy of the order. Quality and robustness depend on conditions such as interdependence, multilateral institutions, norms, soft power, and democratic legitimacy. Legitimacy requires a broader and inclusive set of stakeholders: states, transnational civil society, and corporations, etc. Leadership goes beyond material power and is contingent upon entrepreneurial and intellectual resources, including ideas and innovation. The traditional multilateralism, beholden to American power, Western leadership, inter-governmentalism, and the global level of interaction, gives way to a more inclusive form which is driven by a wider range of actors, issue areas, and levels of interaction. (chapters 3, 4, and 5)

To understand our world in its complexity, we need to add the fourth dimension: time. This dimension speaks to the essential transience of orders, and draws attention to their points of origin and ending. It also reminds us that we cannot replicate past orders, unless someone invents a geopolitical time machine. A good deal of the debate over the post-cold war international order has relied on assumptions and lessons drawn from a Eurocentric historiography (chapter 2). Yet the functioning and outcome of multipolarity or unipolarity in Europe's past offer no definitive clues to the provision of stability for a world which has no historical precedent – that is, the simultaneous rise of a number of states which, while existing in different geographic locations, nonetheless interact on a regular and sustained basis.

Hence, instead of pining for the American-led liberal hegemonic order, we should prepare "to boldly go where no one has gone before."

– 2 –

The Rise and Fall of the Unipolar Moment

The term "unipolar moment" was coined not by an academic, but a media pundit, shortly after the Iraqi invasion of Kuwait in August 1990.[1] It gained considerable popularity in the aftermath of America's resounding victory over Iraqi dictator Saddam Hussein and the expulsion of his occupying forces from Kuwait in early 1991. To be sure, the victorious leader of the coalition forces, US President George H. W. Bush, toned down American dominance and proclaimed a New World Order of multilateralism and international cooperation. As he put it in an address to the US Congress on September 11, 1990, this New World Order would be one "in which the nations of the world, East and West, North and South, can prosper and live in harmony." Krauthammer would unabashedly describe unipolarity as *Pax Americana*. "We have entered a period of Pax Americana. Why deny it? Every other nation would like to be in America's position. Why be embarrassed by it?"[2]

Until then, as the cold war ended, most analysts had initially anticipated multipolarity, both globally and in the important regions of Europe and Asia. John Mearsheimer, an American scholar, foresaw that Europe would go "back to the future" by reviving its pre-world war great-power rivalry. He even expressed nostalgia for the stability afforded by the bipolar system of the cold war.[3] In Asia, Aaron Friedberg, another American scholar, foresaw a multipolar region that would be "ripe for rivalry." For him, Asia's future could resemble Europe's past.[4] By and large, American pundits celebrated the unipolar moment. It was not just another stage in international order, but also a desirable development for America and the world.

The unipolar-moment idea exerted a powerful influence over the academic debate over world order in the post-cold war era. Some American pundits, like Krauthammer himself, were careful not to take unipolarity for granted. It was to be a "moment," rather than an era. Multipolarity would take another generation to arrive. Others, such as William Wohlforth, predicted that unipolarity would be much more durable. As the leading advocate of the "unipolar stability" school, he argued that unipolarity might survive as long as bipolarity, which lasted for nearly four and half decades.[5]

There came another view, which argued that unipolarity was an "illusion." Power balancing, or the tendency of states to band together to challenge a hegemon, is both natural and inevitable, something of a law of international politics. It was a matter of time before other great powers would rise to contest American predominance.[6]

In the end, unipolarity is proving to be rather short-lived. Of course, we have no clear definition of unipolarity to make a precise assessment of when it might end. Wohlforth defines unipolarity as "decisive preponderance in all the underlying components of power: economic, military, technological, and geopolitical."[7] The key word here has to be "decisive." The US is likely to remain as the Number One military power for quite some time. But the US invasion of Iraq in 2003 has shown that superior military power does not translate to geopolitical influence, which is a major requirement for unipolar stability. To be sure, the election of Barrack Obama as US President in 2009 and his foreign policy have reversed some of the anti-Americanism generated by the George W. Bush era of unilateralism. But Obama has not increased US influence internationally.[8] The picture is even less rosy for the US on the economic front. Some forecasts see China overtaking the US as the world's largest economy as early as 2016.[9] While the unipolar moment was for real, it was also more fragile or unstable than its proponents had thought or claimed.

How might unipolarity end? Krauthammer argued that the most serious challenge to unipolarity would not come from competing nations like China. Nor would it come from domestic liberal isolationists still haunted by the memories of Vietnam and opposed to foreign adventures for the sake of promoting American values. Rather it would come from the old-fashioned isolationism of traditional conservatives, who believe that America's national interests are never served by foreign entanglements and adventures of any kind. But Krauthammer was wrong – as he himself was to admit later.[10] It was not the paleo-conservatives but the neo-cons who dominated the foreign policy of the George W. Bush administration, and hastened the end of the unipolar moment. Ironically, they did so by pushing for an aggressive agenda of *Pax Americana* as Krauthammer had envisioned. Krauthammer believed that unipolarity might last as long as America was led by people who avoided the paralyzing affliction of multilateralism and pursued an assertive foreign policy to confront its enemies. Yet it was these very policies under the George W. Bush administration – the toxic combination of unipolarity with unilateralism – that speeded the end of his cherished unipolar moment. The fear that the real threat to unipolarity might be America's failure to keep it going, or "failure to do enough,"[11] were hardly prescient. The real threat to unipolarity was not doing too little, but too much, unilaterally.

For those who argued that the main reason for the end of unipolarity would be the rise of other powers, the real threats have come as much from within as from without. By the late 2000s, America was faced with not just a relative but an absolute decline, fueled not only by the invasion of Iraq but also by internal weaknesses and mismanagement (to be discussed shortly).

Notwithstanding their differences, the two perspectives, which I term as "unipolar illusion" and "unipolar stability," have three things in common. First, both accept that international order is shaped primarily by structural factors, especially the distribution of power.[12] Hence the key to understanding the prospects for peace and stability in the world is polarity – whether the distribution of power is bipolar, multipolar, or unipolar. But the structuralist lens is not a very reliable guide to understanding world order, because it often overlooks the role of domestic politics, international institutions, and normative forces shaping world peace and stability. For example, domestic politics, especially democratization trends around the world, can greatly influence factors of peace and stability. International norms and institutions, too, have been increasingly important in this area. Regional institutions and norms have been especially crucial to stability in Europe and to a lesser but still important extent in Asia. Hence the fate of the unipolar moment depends not just on the changing balance of power, caused by the rise of other great powers, but also on these other forces. Unipolarity can invite resistance and be challenged on normative grounds, as the rising tide of anti-Americanism after the Iraq invasion showed.

Second, structuralist perspectives often take a narrow view of what *stability* means. One of the most prominent structural theorists of international relations, Kenneth Waltz, famously equated bipolarity (e.g., the cold war) with stability and multipolarity (pre-World War II international systems) with volatility and conflict.[13] Bipolarity reduced the scope for misunderstanding, misperception, and confusion among the two superpowers. "In a bipolar world uncertainty lessens and calculations are easier to make."[14] Indeed, by extending "the geographic scope of both [super]powers' concern," bipolarity reduced the possibility of international conflict. Moreover, "the pressures of a bipolar world strongly encourage[d] them [the superpowers] to act internationally in ways better than their characters may lead one to expect."[15] John Lewis Gaddis provided a further elaboration of this view by pointing to the tendency of "self-regulation" in a bipolar relationship. Referring to the willingness and ability of the two superpowers to manage major international crises during the cold war period, Gaddis concludes that this functioned like "the automatic pilot on an airplane or the governor on a steam engine" in counteracting threats to international stability.

What was the meaning of stability here? Waltz first took stability to mean both durability of a situation and peace within it. Later he changed his position and defined stability only as durability of the system. Yet bipolarity ended more quickly than Waltz, or for that matter anyone else, had anticipated. And it was hardly peaceful for a good part of the world. Disciples of Waltz, including Gaddis and Mearsheimer, stressed both virtues of bipolarity. Yet it was a rather thin view of "stability." In his essay "The Long Peace," Gaddis argued "the most convincing argument for 'stability' [of the bipolar world] is that so far at least, World War III has not occurred."[16] But his Waltz-like view of the cold war as a "long peace" was applicable only to Europe or the "central balance"; regional conflicts raged throughout the third world despite, or perhaps because of, the interventionism of the superpowers. As Ayoob argued, local and regional conflicts in the third world were not only more "permissible," but superpower intervention there might have served as a necessary "safety valve" not available in the European context.[17] So, instead of dampening conflicts in the third world, superpower rivalry actually contributed to their escalation, which led to the internationalization of civil war and internalization of superpower competition.

The post-cold war debates over unipolarity take stability to include the peacefulness of the international system. Peace is equated entirely with the absence of systemic or major power war. Both perspectives ignore internal and regional conflicts, alongside intervention in the developing world or the War on Terror. By equating unipolarity with peace, the unipolar stability thesis takes a rather narrow view of stability and ignores the horrific regional conflicts that ravaged the Balkans, the Great Lakes region of Africa, East Timor, Iraq and Afghanistan after the 9/11 attacks, and the War on Terror, among others. Internal and local conflicts or collateral damage from the War on Terror were not regarded as threats to peace. Both the unipolar stability and unipolar illusion perspectives, which embrace the realist view of international relations, believe that the end of unipolarity would mean heightened global disorder.[18] What is more interesting is that a similar equation between peace and the preponderance of American power can be found in liberal perspectives on world order. Hence the claim by some American liberal theorists (to be discussed in the next chapter) that the American-led liberal hegemony order (a form of unipolarity albeit legitimized through American strategic restraint and American-inspired multilateral institutions) has been largely peace-inducing and that its end would mean instability and disorder in the international system.

Third, structuralist perspectives on world order are often based on evidence that is heavily Eurocentric. Much of the evidence behind Mearsheimer's "back to the future" prognosis for Europe after the cold war, as well as Friedbeg's "ripe for rivalry" outlook for Asia, came from Europe before World War II. The evidence for "unipolar illusion," that is, the transience of unipolarity and the rise of challengers, also comes from Europe based on the response to the rise of France in the later seventeenth century and of Britain in the late eighteenth century. The argument for unipolar stability is made by showing how the current unipolarity under the US is distinct from past situations where the concentration of power was the greatest – for example, 1860–70 (Britain in Europe), and 1945–55 (the cold war). Wohlforth expects us to believe that because unipolarity is more real this time around, durable peace would be more likely.

While debates over the unipolar moment revolved around lessons drawn from Western history and geopolitics (European and cold war as applied to the "central strategic balance"), the world is fast moving toward a situation with no historical precedent, i.e., the simultaneous rise of a number of states existing in different geographic locations which nonetheless interact on a regular and sustained basis. While individual great powers had existed in different parts of the world throughout history, they were always in relative isolation from each other. Globalization, with the attendant transport and communication revolutions, new power projection technologies, and the emergence of global institutions and norms, and transnational actors (both positive players like human rights advocacy groups and dark forces like transnational criminal gangs) now make it possible, and indeed imperative, for great powers to interact in a sustained manner to affect international order globally. The result is a world that can hardly be described in terms of the traditional Eurocentric historiography of polarity. By the time the world was catching up to this realization, partly as the result of another overblown narrative about the "rise of the Rest," one important factor in the traditional discourse of American hegemony was making a last stand, which could be called a theory of the liberal hegemonic order, or hegemony without a hegemon.

Without necessarily defending the structuralist view of international order, it is worth pointing out that an increase in the number of great powers does not necessarily spell chaos and disorder in the international system. Waltz contrasted the stability-inducing attributes of bipolarity with the dangers inherent in a multipolar system. In a "multipolar world, who is a danger to whom is often unclear;

the incentive to regard all disequilibrating changes with concern and respond to them with whatever effort may be required is consequently weakened."[19] Mearsheimer holds that while "a bipolar system has only one dyad across which war might break out," a "multipolar system is much more fluid and has many such dyads," thereby making war more likely.[20]

Yet, even from a strictly realist standpoint, having a several powers in an international system could inhibit conflict. Copeland suggests that multipolar systems may be less prone to war because the would-be aggressor cannot be sure about its countervailing coalition.[21] It also inhibits aggression by increasing the size and power of its potentially countervailing coalition. To take a contemporary example, the only Asian power with a potential for undertaking significant territorial expansion, China, is checked not only by the US but also by Japan and India. Deterrence may thus be easier in multipolarity because there are more states that can join together to confront an especially aggressive state with overwhelming force.[22] Deutsch and Singer argue that in multipolarity "the share of attention that any nation can devote to any other must of necessity diminish." Hence conflicts in peripheral areas would have a limited potential for escalation.[23] Multipolarity in their view is also likely to have a "dampening effect upon arms races."[24]

The existence of multiple powers may also induce greater international cooperation. Deutsch and Singer point out that having multiple great powers increases "the range and flexibility of interactions" in an international system.[25] Increased opportunities for interaction create cross-pressures on the strategic designs of the great power, and may lead to cross-cutting interest formation. One power's hostility toward a member of a rival strategic coalition may be balanced by positive feelings toward other members of that same coalition. For a contemporary example, China's competitive instincts versus America may be tempered by its desire for good relations with Pakistan or the Southeast Asian countries, which are closer to the US. Multipolarity may also promote pluralistic common interests,[26] leading to cooperation, as happened in the early nineteenth-century European Concert system.

Furthermore, those debating the unipolar moment seem oblivious to the fact that there can be a significant disjuncture between the global and regional distributions of power.[27] A regional tripolarity in Asia obtained during much of the cold war bipolarity. Different regions may exhibit different types of power distribution. Even if the unipolar moment or American hegemony persists at the global level, it will almost certainly coexist with a multipolar or bipolar regional order in Asia. Hence a prognosis about stability, made with the global distribution of power in mind, may not necessarily capture the dynamics of regional security orders. The problem is compounded by the difficulty of assessing polarity in a critical region like Asia. Is Asia's emerging order unipolar, bipolar, or multipolar? All three scenarios have been suggested in the past two decades.[28] Although the Chinese officially seek to promote global multipolarity, cynics argue that their real goal may be regional unipolarity. Asia's future regional power structure could well be a bipolar one, while multipolarity prevails at the global level. These uncertainties make predictions about stability based mainly on the distribution of power at the global level unconvincing. They also call for serious attention to the state of regional orders.

The Fall and Rise of Declinism

The relationship between unipolarity and international stability was central to the debate over world order as the cold war ended. There was no serious reckoning of the US decline in this debate. The "unipolar moment" had eclipsed Paul Kennedy's argument about the American decline as presented in his *The Rise and Fall of the Great Powers* in 1987.[29] His "imperial overstretch" argument was buried in the rubble of the Berlin Wall. The term "emerging powers" had not emerged yet; this was well before Goldman Sachs coined "BRICs" in 2001. But since the US invasion of Iraq in 2003, the discussion of American power and world order has focused not so much on polarity, but more on the fate and future of American hegemony. This debate is much more about the rise of the Rest and the decline of the West.

At the outset, a caveat about the American decline debate: the claim about American decline, wrote columnist Ezra Kline, is "maddeningly vague." As he continues, "What does it mean for the U.S. to be in decline? Are we talking about our geopolitical influence relative to other world powers? Our standard of living relative to other nations? Our current standard of living compared with some assumption about its appropriate rate of improvement?"[30]

There are three main differences between the latest "America in decline" debate, and the previous one triggered by the Paul Kennedy thesis. The debate based on the latter was mainly over the costs and consequences of America's geopolitical overextension. The current decline debate is over a much wider variety of possible causes: domestic and external, such as the tax cuts, current account deficits, diffusion of technology around the world, gridlock governance, doubts over US ability to pay off its debts, Moody's downgrading of the US, growing health-care costs, forecasts of a debt/GDP ratio by 2016 that is over 100 percent, and the consequent doubts over the status of the dollar as reserve currency.[31] There was, of course, an echo of Kennedy's overstretch argument; the Afghan and Iraq wars, dubbed as the most expensive wars in US history, have a price tag of US $6 trillion in total direct and indirect costs. Iraq alone cost $2 trillion in direct government expenditures.[32]

Second, while external forces and competition figured in both debates, this time the main rival has not been Japan or Germany, but China and the other emerging powers, some of which were not even on the horizon then. In 1987, when the Paul Kennedy book was published, China's reform was less than a decade old. India's had not started. In 1987, China GDP was 678,661 million (or 0.6 trillion). In 2012, it was 12.4 trillion (in purchasing power parity terms). In 1987, China ranked 9th in the world in GDP. Today, it is Number Two.

Third, the previous decline debate came amidst the optimism of the Reagan economic revival. Reagan's "it's morning again in America" advertisement, which appeared during his campaign for re-election, easily overshadowed the idea of a superpower in eclipse. Not surprisingly, that decline debate was short-lived. Its last vestiges disappeared with the US victory over Saddam Hussein and the collapse of the Soviet Union, both of which occurred in 1991. The new decline debate took off after the early "mission accomplished" optimism of George W. Bush quickly gave way to the Vietnam-like feel of an Iraq quagmire, and the rapid transformation of a Clinton surplus to a historic deficit. Hence, this time around, the objective signs of a superpower under strain were palpably visible. The wave of anti-Americanism triggered by George W. Bush's foreign-policy unilateralism compounded that perception by adding a soft power deficit. This may explain why this time the debate has lingered on.

Like the previous one, the new decline of America thesis has sparked a vigorous debate among American politicians and pundits. A good deal of this debate revolves around three areas, which may be summarized as: the "crying wolf" syndrome, the "bionic man" argument, and the "Roman Empire" analogy.

The "crying wolf" pits those who dismiss the notion of decline because they have heard it all before, against those who think this time the "wolf" has indeed arrived. The "bionic man" argument is between those who say the US economy and hence influence will recover soon enough, versus those who say that it will not matter because this decline is mainly relative and the US competitors will do better and catch up faster. The Roman Empire analogy has been presented by Joseph Nye, a leading figure in the anti-declinist camp. Nye contends that the US decline, if it occurs at all, would be like that of the Roman Empire. It will be in slow motion. The obvious counter-argument here, of course, is that it did not take Britain that long to decline from its superpower perch and that the Roman Empire did not have any real imperial rival (it fell, as Nye correctly points out, to the barbarians through a thousand cuts) until the Eastern empire in Constantinople found one in the Ottoman Turks. Unlike the Roman Empire, but like the British in the early twentieth century, the US as the reigning but weakening hegemon does face some serious challengers, not the least of which is China. Hence its downfall may not take as long as the 200 plus years it took the Roman Empire to wither.

To ardent anti-declinists like Robert Kagan, the current concerns about America's decline resemble those after World War I or during the 1970s, with the Vietnam War, both of which were also times of economic hardship. It is nothing new; just a sign of a "neurotic" superpower nation.[33] Yet he points out that America's share of the world's GDP has remained at around 25 percent since the early 1970s.[34] However, Robert Pape of the University of Chicago argues that the US has experienced one of the most significant declines of any state since the mid-nineteenth century. Using IMF data and constant 2000 US dollars as the measure (whereas Kagan's US Department of Agriculture data uses a latter constant dollar measure),[35] Pape calculates that the US share of the world GDP fell by 7.7 percent from 2000 to 2008, from 31 percent to 23.1 percent, a not insignificant decline. In the corresponding period, China's share of the world GDP grew from 2 to 7 percent.[36] Speaking of the "crying wolf," Gideon Rachman of the *Financial Times* remarks, "a frequently overlooked fact about that fable is that the boy was eventually proved right. The wolf did arrive – and China is the wolf."[37]

Some anti-declinists argue that it is not in the US, but in Europe and Japan that the real decline has occurred. In fact, the US share of the world GDP was largely maintained because of the drop in Western Europe and Japan. Hence, "It is this trilateral system – rather than American power per se – that is in decline today," argues Walter Russell Mead.[38] But others such as Clyde Prestowitz question the view that America's economic performance for the past two decades has been that much superior to those of its allies. The periods of high growth in the late 1990s and between 2002 and 2008 were actually two "highly destructive bubbles." And because of higher rates of population growth and inflation in the US, and the different ways of counting productivity in US and Japan, the performances of America and Japan for past 20 years are not "terribly different . . . if Japan has stagnated, so has America."[39] Furthermore, even the relative success of the American economy vis-à-vis Europe and Japan cannot be a matter of consolation for the US, because of what Kupchan calls the "collective aspect to US hegemony." Because the US hegemony is so closely founded on that trilateral system, for example, the involvement and support of Europe and Japan, their predicament can hardly be good for America.[40]

Another argument against the thesis for the decline of America holds that even if the emerging powers acquire growing wealth relative to America, it would not necessarily translate into greater power or influence. Citing the case of India, Kagan argues that even if India has become economically better off today, its international influence might have suffered compared to the 1950s and 1960s, when it was poorer but a leader of the non-aligned movement.[41] It is true that India then enjoyed a good deal of international prestige, much of it due to its inspirational non-violent struggle for independence from British rule, but also because of Jawaharlal Nehru's personal charisma and active diplomacy. But much of it was also premised on the hope of other postcolonial nations that India would

succeed and show the way through its economic development agenda. When India failed to do so, and after other
Asian nations posted superior economic performance,
India's international influence dived. (Some other factors
also contributed to this: defeat in the 1962 war with China,
domestic instability, strains in alliances with the West over
its close ties with the Soviet Bloc, etc.). India is not really
that rich as yet, as Kagan assumes, and its political influence
had actually recovered since the economic reforms began in
the early 1990s and put it into the ranks of the emerging
powers. And if India's economy continues to perform, there
is every possibility that its global influence will increase, and
it will assume a seat at the table of leading nations of the
twenty-first century. In fact there is no other route for the
achievement of its global status and influence.

According to the optimistic view of America's future,
the rise of the wealth or military capability of other nations
makes the demand for US leadership even stronger. Nye
argues, "As India, Japan, and others try to balance Chinese
power, they will increasingly welcome an American presence."[42] There is some evidence of this in Asia, where
several countries in China's neighborhood are reaching out
to Washington for closer political and security ties. Yet the
situation is far more complex than Nye presents it to be.
The courting of Washington is not a foregone conclusion.
It depends not on China's rising power per se, but on
actual Chinese foreign policy and security behavior. Indeed,
most of the Asian nations did not seek to balance China
until it abandoned its "charm offensive" and turned assertive in 2009. This coincided with the US "pivot" to Asia,
induced partly by the Chinese challenge, as well as the
impending withdrawals from Iraq and Afghanistan. This
was a push factor behind the seeming willingness of Asian
nations to welcome the US presence (it was presented to
them as a fait accompli). Yet Asians do not welcome
intensified Sino–US competition; for them, as some
might put it, "too much rebalancing may be as bad as
too little."

To be sure, arguments that the emerging powers such as India, China, Brazil, Mexico, Turkey, and so on have their economic, military, and political shortcomings must be factored in while assessing the matter of America's relative decline. The challenges confronting the new powers include the likelihood of catching the "middle-income trap" (a point where growth becomes noticeably slower, as happened in the case of Japan, South Korea, and Taiwan),[43] domestic instability, lower population growth, embroilment in regional conflicts, and so on. In contrast, the US still enjoys fundamental domestic and external strengths, such as its universities, its lead in science and innovation, its openness to immigration, its alliances around the world, and its commitment to multilateralism, which, we are often reminded, is after all an *American* institution. While differentiating absolute decline from relative, Nye points out that the US economy remains highly productive, and the country is "first in the world in total research and development spending, first in university rankings, first in Nobel Prizes, and first on indices of entrepreneurship," and the world's seventh most competitive economy, while China is 29th. "This is hardly a picture of absolute economic decline."[44] But the picture is not all that rosy on the absolute decline front, with rising income inequality, declining infrastructure, and the transformation of the US from being the world's largest creditor nation to being its largest debtor.[45] With a projected population growth of more than 100 million by 2050, and a labor-force increase of 40 percent, the US is likely to enjoy an advantage in population growth relative to China (which will have both a growing senior population and a declining workforce), Russia, and Europe.[46] And US military strength has not suffered, at least not as yet, judging by its defense-spending levels. That spending grew from being 1.7 times the military spending by all non-US NATO members in 2000, to being more than twice that in 2010; and from being seven times higher than Chinese defense spending in 2000, to nine times higher in 2010.[47] But Chinese military spending is also growing in absolute terms alongside its key defense capabilities, such as long-range nuclear missiles and area denial capabilities.[48] At the same time, the US is already cutting back its defense spending due to budgetary pressures and the withdrawals from Iraq and Afghanistan. Overall, while these relative strengths of the US in education, population, and the military are important, do they justify President Obama's assertion, in his 2012 State of the Union address, that "Anyone who tells you that America is in decline or that our influence has waned, doesn't know what they're talking about"?

They do not, at least if one looks at the issue of decline in relative terms. The US GDP relative to China's has declined from being eight times higher in 2000 to less than three times higher in 2010. And, despite the growth of the US economy in that decade, it fell by 19 percent relative to the G-20 countries as a whole.[49] While the developing countries continue to face the challenge of poverty and inequality and a technology and infrastructure gap vis-à-vis the West, the changing economic balance between the North and the South is a marked feature of the emerging world order and a key basis of the Multiplex world. This has major implications for the direction of the global economy, and the future of Western dominance and endurance of the America-led liberal order. The developing countries are set to account for nearly 60 percent of world GDP by 2030.[50] The share of developing countries in the global economy has increased dramatically in the past decade relative to the West. Estimates of gross national income (GNI) for 2009, released on July 1, showed that the share of developing regions in the global economy increased from 18 percent in 2000 to 28 percent in 2009. On a purchasing power parity (PPP) basis, their share increased from 34 to 44 percent, with China becoming the second largest economy after the United States. Brazil, Russia, India, and Mexico are among the 15 largest economies in the world.[51] By 2060, the combined GDP of China (27.8 percent) and India (18.2 percent) will be larger than that of the OECD – and the total output of China, India, and the rest of the developing world (57.7 percent) will be greater than that of developed OECD and non-OECD countries (42.3 percent).[52]

Surely, even some Western estimates, such as the two reports on global trends for 2030 produced by the Paris-based European Union Institute for Security Studies (EUISS), the EU's official (although it counts itself as "autonomous") agency for the analysis of foreign, security, and defense policy issues, and the US National Intelligence Council (NIC), an official arm of the US government (under the Director of National Intelligence), would question Obama's optimism, at least under some scenarios.

The EUISS report, entitled *Global Trends 2030*, (hereafter referred to as the *EUISS 2030 Report*),[53] offers an interesting classification of the global power structure in 2030. The US, the European Union, China, India, and Brazil are listed as great powers; Russia and Japan are described as uncertain great powers ("uncertainty for some great powers"); under the category "rising middle powers" are listed Indonesia, South Africa, Turkey, Mexico, Germany, Britain, and France. Finally, Nigeria, Pakistan, Egypt, and Iran are dubbed as uncertain middle powers. The five largest economies of the world (in terms of share in global GDP) in 2030 would be China (23.8 percent), the US (17.3 percent), the EU (14.3 percent), India (10.4 percent), and Japan (3.5 percent).

According to the *EUISS 2030 Report*, the US will very likely remain the major military power in 2030, although it will suffer a relative decline and become unable to sustain the present level of military expenditure (currently 4.8 percent of its GDP). The US will also be the only country with a global military outreach. However, it is likely that it will project military power primarily through broader coalitions, except where vital national interests are threatened or in response to a direct attack, in which case unilateral action is always an option. By 2030, China may have become not only the major economic power but also the country with the largest share of material power. China is likely to have the world's strongest aerospace power two decades from now, and it may become a leading military force. Its current long-term military expenditure program will give it a powerful defensive capability and a very predominant regional role, but it will probably not be in a position to project power decisively beyond the Asia-Pacific region. China and India are likely to increase their populations from 1.3 to 1.4 billion and 1.2 to 1.5 billion citizens respectively by 2030. Together, China and India will account for 34 percent of the global economy, respectively forming the first and fourth largest world economies in 2030. The NIC's *Global Trends 2030 Report* (hereafter called *The NIC 2030 Report*), released in December 2013, projects that by 2030 Asia will have surpassed North America and Europe combined in terms of global power, based upon GDP, population size, military spending, and technological investment. But even under the "most optimistic scenario," the relative size of the US economy would decline from about a third of the combined GDP of the G-20 countries in 2010 to about a quarter of it in 2030 in real US dollars. While the US economy would remain the world's largest at market exchange rates, the report foresees China surpassing the US a few years before 2030 to become the world's largest economy (in PPP terms). America's share of world trade would dip from around 12 percent to 10 percent, while East Asia's share would probably double from 10 percent to 20 percent. The sharpest indicator of the US decline would be the end of the US dollar as the global reserve currency and its replacement by another or a basket of currencies. But this is less likely to happen. The health of the global economy would depend more on the economic performance of the developing world – China, India, Brazil, Colombia, Indonesia, Nigeria, South Africa, and Turkey, etc. – than of the Western countries. Remarkably, the report sees India outperforming China, whose economy is projected to slow down by 2030.

The *NIC 2030 Report* also projects that the US will "remain the single most powerful country" in the world because "No other power would be likely to achieve the same panoply of power in this time frame under any plausible scenario." The US would still be "called upon" to act as a balancer to China in Asia. But the report confirms the relative decline of the US:

> The US most likely will remain "first among equals" among the other great powers in 2030 because of its preeminence across a range of power dimensions and legacies of its leadership role. More important than just its economic weight, the United States' dominant role in international politics has derived from its preponderance across the board in both hard and soft power. Nevertheless, with the rapid rise of other countries, the "unipolar moment" is over and Pax Americana – the era of American ascendancy in international politics that began in 1945 – is fast winding down.[54]

Another recent study, commissioned by the Asian Development ment Bank, (hereafter called the *Asia 2050 Report*), paints two scenarios. The first, called the "Asian century," foresees Asia's share of global GDP reaching 39.9 percent in 2030, and 52.3 percent in 2050. China alone will account for 20 percent of the global GDP, and India 16 percent. By comparison, the US will account for 12 percent. Asia's combined GDP will be 174 trillion, with China accounting for 68 trillion and India 53 trillion (in US dollars and market exchange rates). The US will account for $38 trillion. Asia's per capita income will reach $20,000 in 2030 and $37,300 in 2050, compared to the world average of $37,000. A key assumption of this scenario is that the 11 fastest-growing economies in Asia of the past 30 years will continue to grow for the next 40 years, and that a sizeable portion (40 percent) of the slow and modest growth countries in Asia will converge toward the higher growth of the top 11.

But under the second scenario, Asia's growing economies will fall into the "middle-income trap" within the next two decades, thereby following the pattern of Latin America over the past 30 years. Asia's share of the global GDP will be 31 percent, with China accounting for 10 percent and India 7 percent, compared to 18 percent for the US. Asia's combined GDP will be $65 trillion, China's $20 trillion, India's $14 trillion, and America's $38 trillion. Per capita GDP under this scenario would be $20,600 for Asia as a whole, $23,500 for China, $17,900 for India, and $25,600 for the world. The US per capita income is estimated at $94,900.[55]

Despite all their differences, however, there are two areas that unite the believers and skeptics when it comes to the issue of the US decline. First, no major Western analyst or analysis accepts that the US decline might be good for international order either in general or in specific areas such as development, governance, and international justice. The overall consensus seems to be that the loss of American predominance results in heightened international instability. For liberals, the US decline means a reduction in the international leadership needed to organize international cooperation and conflict management. For realists, it may lead to conflict because declining powers tend to become targets of opportunistic aggression by rival powers and coalitions, or themselves become aggressive.

Even critics of the durability of unipolarity (the realist unipolar illusion perspective) think that its end will spell heightened international rivalry. And just like the realists, the liberals also believe that such an end would mean danger, disorder, and disintegration. The consequences of the loss of America's pre-eminence would be that "[i]nsecure sea lanes, impoverished trading partners, exorbitant oil prices, explosive regional instability are only the more obvious risks of an American abdication."[56] Even Layne, who is skeptical of unipolarity, fears that its inevitable end would mean "traditional patterns of great power competition will reemerge," including the possibility of hegemonic war (incredibly, for someone writing in the early 1990s, he thought of Japan rather than China as the likely challenger to the US).[57] Ikenberry could foresee "less desirable alternatives" to the liberal hegemonic order, "great-power-balancing orders, regional blocs, or bipolar rivalries."[58]

Second, and related to the above, it is hard to find any mainstream American writer who would vote for anything other than maintaining continued US primacy, even though some would not want to see the return of the George W. Bush era of unipolar unilateralism. While some may still be in denial, others accept decline with a fair deal of reluctance. And almost everyone seeks revival and restitution, prescribing steps as to how the US might restore its pre-eminence.

− 3 −
The Myths of Liberal Hegemony

One distinctive view of the changing world order argues that whether or not America is in decline, the order it has created would persist and might even co-opt its main challengers, including China. This view[1] rests on three main elements. First, it posits the existence of an American-led "liberal hegemonic order and the acquiescence and support of other states" to this since the end of World War II. (As noted in chapter 1, I have used the term "American-led liberal hegemonic order" interchangeably with the "American World Order," or AWO). Second, this order is facing three main challenges: the rise of unipolarity, eroded norms of state sovereignty, and the shifting sources of violence, all resulting in "a crisis of authority." Third, the liberal hegemonic order is far from finished. No alternatives to it have emerged. On the contrary, "the rise of non-Western powers and the growth of economic and security interdependence are creating new constituencies and pressures for liberal international order."[2]

The first of the three challenges to the AWO is already passé. The real challenge to that order is not the rise of unipolarity, which has eroded rapidly, but its end, with the rise of a number of powers. The AWO has some distinct echoes of the notion of hegemony developed by the Italian Marxist Antonio Gramsci. Gramsci theorized that a hegemony is upheld more through the consent than the coercion of the governed, at least of the elite among the latter.[3] But, ultimately, the Gramscian concept views hegemony unflatteringly due to its tendency to breed inequality and injustice, and calls for the mobilization of popular resistance to it with alternative ideas and approaches. By contrast, the liberal hegemony thesis glorifies hegemonic rule, and paints a dark picture of its alternatives.

More importantly, the AWO also has a close affinity with the hegemonic stability theory (HST) and may even be regarded as an updated refinement of it.[4] According to a well-known description by Isabelle Grunberg, the HST holds that "cooperation and a well-functioning world economy are dependent on a certain kind of political structure, a structure characterized by the dominance of a single actor . . . Both Great Britain in the nineteenth century and the United States after World War II helped bring about an interdependent and overall peaceful world."[5] Ikenberry argues that "Great Britain in the nineteenth century, with its non-empire-related capacity as a champion of free trade and open navigation, and the United States after World War II are the great historical cases of liberal hegemony."[6]

In HST, a hegemon creates international economic or security institutions to serve its own self-interest, but these institutions are also in harmony with the interests of others, and thus serve an altruistic purpose. A hegemon maintains such regimes by coercion or through incentives to followers.[7] The hegemon's rule seeks to discourage cheating and encourage others to share the costs of maintaining the system. As noted, however, compared to the HST, the AWO downplays the coercion aspect.

The HST originated in and captured the historical context of the inter-war period, a period of transition between the British and the American hegemony. It was essentially a story about the emergence and consequences of American hegemony. Despite attracting criticism as a self-serving and ethnocentric American concept,[8] and for its limited ability to explain order and change in world politics induced by other actors and forces (such as normative ideas),[9] the HST has proven to be remarkably durable. It has been used to give credit to the US in the creation of new economic and security institutions like the GATT, IMF, World Bank, and the UN after World War II. Like Britain, the US benefitted from free trade, while offering incentives to lesser states which in turn benefitted from access to the US market and security protection from the American security umbrella.

The HST constitutes a powerful metanarrative of the evolution of the contemporary international order. A metanarrative means a "big story," or a "high-level theory," and "a perspective/ideology."[10] It is "a theory that tries to give a totalizing, comprehensive account to various historical events, experiences, and social, cultural phenomena based upon the appeal to universal truth or universal values." As such, a metanarrative "functions to legitimize power, authority, and social customs."[11] As Grunberg suggests, the endurance of HST had to do with the fact that it is "comprehensive" or "so elegant while at the same time encompassing so much."[12] This durability and the conceptual connection between HST and AWO vindicate those who viewed the former as a "fantasy" that captured the "American political imagination" and that "lingers in the mind long after it has proven fallacious."[13]

Given this affinity, some of the criticisms of HST may well apply to the AWO, especially the tendency to simplify reality. But the AWO's credibility faces a special problem, one that concerns its geographic scope. What is the liberal hegemonic order? Ikenberry describes it in the following terms:

At its core, it was a hierarchical order with liberal characteristics. America played the leading role in the provision of rule and stability in that order. It was a hierarchical system that was built on both American power dominance and liberal principles of governance. The United States was the dominant state, but its power advantages were muted and mediated by an array of postwar rules, institutions, and reciprocal political processes – backed up by shared strategic interests and political bargains. Weaker and secondary states were given institutionalized access to the exercise of American power. The United States provided public goods and operated within a loose system of multilateral rules and institutions. American hegemonic power and liberal international order were fused – indeed they each were dependent on the other.[14]

This definition carefully avoids any explicit reference to the geographic reach or memberships (or stakeholdership) of that order. In delineating its scope, we are not helped by the fact that Ikenberry in his *Liberal Leviathan*, quoted above, calls it by several names: "liberal hegemonic order" (xi, 224); "American-led liberal world order" (xii); "American-led liberal hegemony" (224); "free world, the American system, the West, the Atlantic world, Pax Democratica, Pax Americana, the Philadelphia system" (35). We may look for the broadest of these terms, although it is difficult to know which one would qualify. The "American-led liberal hegemonic order" perhaps?

In any case, each of these terms raises questions and some designations contradict others. For example, "Atlantic world" may be the most precise way of defining the liberal order, but it is also too narrow, geographically speaking at least. What about Australia and New Zealand? If Pax Democratica is used, what about South Korea and Taiwan before democratization, and Singapore even today? To be sure, these states were drawn into the liberal order by the force of economic necessity and security geopolitics. But can we consider them as members of the liberal hegemonic order because of their capitalist economic systems and their dependence on the US market and the American security umbrella, even though they did not have its most fundamental defining value: a genuinely democratic political system?

The notion of the "free world" fares no better. Given its ideologically charged origin as a tool of Western cold war propaganda, it is really surprising that this term would figure in any serious academic definition and discussion about world order, past or future. It made sense if narrowly applied to the "West" during the cold war, but not beyond. Was India, the world's largest democracy, where genuine freedom of expression prevailed and there was no American-style McCarthyism, ever a part of the "free world"? Most Indians, certainly its first prime minister, Jawaharlal Nehru, would have cringed at being so labeled. How about "the West"? Although this term is slightly less obsolete than the "free world," it is even more limited (including the near absurdity of encompassing Japan within the category), divisive, and just as ideologically specific. Compared to "free world" or "the West," or "the Atlantic," "American-led liberal hegemonic order" seems more apt. But it too raises important questions regarding its scope, ideological bias, and credibility. I outline four myths of liberal hegemony, hence of the AWO, below.

The first myth concerns the question of how far the "American-led liberal hegemonic order" actually extended for much of its history, especially during the cold war period. The answer is obvious: only a small part of the world was influenced by this concept. The Soviet Bloc, China, India, Indonesia, and a good part of the "third world" were outside of it. Despite the exalted claims about its power, legitimacy, and public good functions, that order was little more than the US-UK-West Europe-Australasian configuration.

Let us consider three countries that were not part of the liberal hegemonic order for much of the cold war. In 1960 the Soviet Union was producing 12.5 percent of the world's goods (from farm and factory), just under half that of the United States (25.9 percent) and the European Economic Community (26 percent). These figures had changed little by 1970.[15] The Soviet Union represented 14.31 percent of the world's economy in 1969 (its highest point) and occupied a sixth of the land area of the world. Its arable land alone was equal to that of the United States and Canada combined. China and India weighed less heavily on the global economic front during the cold war, but India, which represented 3.1 percent of the world's economy in 1964 (its highest point), also happened to be the world's largest democracy. And it chose to be an ally of the USSR. Jawaharlal Nehru and his daughter (who also became the Indian prime minister), Indira Gandhi, were among the leading critics of American foreign policy during their times. At the first conference of postcolonial nations, three of Asia's largest and most populous nations – China, India, and Indonesia – rejected key elements of the liberal hegemonic order, including one of its then principal elements, the alliance known as the Southeast Asia Treaty Organization (SEATO). Egypt, another influential member of the postcolonial nations, joined them in rejecting the Baghdad Pact.

As such, the American-led liberal hegemonic order can be viewed as *an* international order, but not *the* world order, of the post-World War II period, right until the end of the cold war. At the very least, it existed alongside the overarching cold war order, which both subsumed it and subverted its purpose by often pushing the US into sacrificing liberal norms, such as human rights and democracy in allied third-world nations, and undermining the UN's peace and security role in the interest of superpower geopolitics.

The collapse of the USSR and the Soviet Bloc, the democratization and economic reorientation of Eastern European countries toward the West, and economic reforms in China, India, and Vietnam, might have expanded the scope of the liberal order after the 1990s. This does not, however, mean the liberal order became uncontested or uncontestable. Plenty of societies and states, not only in the Islamic world or during the George W. Bush presidency, have challenged its ideological underpinnings and questioned its benefits. Moreover, its narrow historical scope at the point of origin and expansion means some of the new entrants into this order lack a sense of ownership. Their absence at the creation of these policies may shape their future affinity with the order. For example, the fact that India and China were not part of the original construction of the liberal hegemonic order is not irrelevant here. India and China accounted for between 50 percent and 60 percent of the world economy for the first 1,500 years AD.[16] And they are projected to account for about 40 percent of the world output by 2050.

The above points lead to a second myth about AWO and the liberal hegemony thesis. This concerns the claim that "the British and American-led liberal orders have been built in critical respects around consent."[17] In reality, coercion and contestation has been the name of the game, unless one views British colonialism as a form of consent. From the colonial period to the post-cold war era, the liberal order has been imposed through coercion – economic, political, and military. Indeed, contestations over key aspects of that order have taken place even within the West: for example, European protests over the War on Terror and the US invasion of Iraq. The fact that these challenges to British or American hegemony did not always prevail does not mean they were absent.

Hence, challenges to and contestations about the liberal hegemonic order are developing not because of the "rise of unipolarity, eroded norms of state sovereignty and shifting sources of violence."[18] They have always been around. Moreover, the "crisis of authority"[19] of the liberal hegemonic order is not the handiwork of al-Qaeda and the George W. Bush administration's "illiberal hegemony."[20] It is not that things were going generally fine until then. The fact is that the liberal hegemonic order has always been contested. These challenges have their basis in more than terrorism or the erosion of the norms of Westphalian sovereignty,[21] for they have also been about issues of economic inequality and injustice, geopolitical expansion and intervention, and the abuse of international institutions to serve the narrow ends of the hegemon. Closely related to the above is a third myth about the AWO, one that concerns claims about the benevolent nature of the liberal hegemonic order. In her "New American Moment" speech at the Council on Foreign Relations in September 2010, Hillary Clinton noted:

> After the Second World War, the nation that had built the transcontinental railroad, the assembly line and the skyscraper turned its attention to constructing the pillars of global cooperation. The third World War that so many feared never came. And many millions of people were lifted out of poverty and exercised their human rights for the first time. Those were the benefits of a global architecture forged over many years by American leaders from both political parties.[22]

The benefits of the AWO deserve due recognition. Ikenberry lists the public goods provided by the order as "in the areas of security provision, maintenance of economic openness and stability, and support for the rules and institutions that formed the order,"[23] although he concedes that those benefits sometimes did not apply to US relations with the developing world. Even American analysts who are highly skeptical of the capacity of US primacy to endure into the future concede its past role in inducing global peace and prosperity, transforming Europe, creating stable global trade and financial regimes – benefits that are especially striking when measured against the record of the Soviet Bloc.[24] Yet the proponents of the liberal hegemony are just too effusive regarding its positives and too silent on the negatives. One does not have to be a Mahathir Mohamad, Fidel Castro, or Noam Chomsky to recognize that the American-led liberal hegemonic order was not so benign for many outside of it, especially in the developing world. At the very least, it projects a mixed picture. Driven by the imperative of the cold war, it was marked by indifference or even opposition to decolonization (as revealed during the Eisenhower administration's efforts to subvert the conference of Asian and African nations in Bandung, Indonesia, in 1955),[25] support for authoritarian rule (Iran, Pakistan, South Korea, Taiwan, Indonesia, etc.), direct or indirect military intervention (e.g., Iran, Vietnam, Cuba, Nicaragua, etc.), and selective support for and hostility to the regional and international multilateralism of the developing nations (including a preference for bilateralism in Asia over multilateralism and downright hostility toward the global non-aligned movement of the third world). Nor did it do a stellar job of preventing and managing conflict in the third world. This historical baggage of the liberal order affects its legitimacy. The dark side of that order had invited resistance well before the "crisis" of that order under the George W. Bush presidency.

A fourth myth about the AWO relates to its sweeping assertions on the benevolent role of the US in constructing global order. These may be exaggerated. At the same time, the contribution of other actors to global peace and order may be understated. Even liberal ideas and norms about global and regional order have not always been "made in America," but developed by others and hence marked by differences and variations among their proponents. As Miles Kahler argues, "other societies played an often unremarked role in creating and sustaining the post-1945 liberal order . . . the American variant of liberalism often failed to represent the spectrum of international liberal norms." He argues, moreover, that the US interpretation of liberal norms after 1945 "often represented a distinctive and controversial interpretation."[26] The West Europeans (independently of the erstwhile hegemonic power, Britain) recognized the limits of sovereignty and nationalism and developed the first supranational bodies of the post-war period. Indeed, the idea of a "pluralistic liberal world order" is more genuine and defensible than the monistic vision of a liberal hegemonic order.[27] The view that there may be other sources and interpretations of liberal norms is significant as it gives more space and sense of ownership to other actors, including the emerging powers, to appropriate and develop those norms. But these are likely to go through adaptations or "localizations," in keeping with the general pattern of norm diffusion in world politics.[28]

The developing countries have also contributed to the development of global norms and governance. The role of the Latin American countries in the nineteenth and early twentieth centuries in developing and deploying a robust and legalistic form of the non-intervention principle (especially against the US Monroe doctrine) should count as an important contribution to the early construction of the global sovereignty regime, and hence to global order building.[29] In the early post-World War II period, Latin Americans were on the forefront of the development of global human rights norms, especially through their intervention at the San Francisco Conference on the UN Charter in 1945, and through the development of early regional mechanisms such as the American Declaration on Human Rights and Duties in April 1948, about 10 months before the UN General Assembly adopted the Universal Declaration on Human Rights.[30] In a recent study, Eric Helleiner demonstrates that non-Western countries – Latin American and Eastern European countries states as well as China and India – played a significant role in "shaping and supporting" the creation of the post-war global economic institutions, including Bretton Woods, the International Monetary Fund (IMF), and the World Bank. They were especially crucial in injecting and strengthening the development role of these institutions. As he puts it, "The Bretton Woods negotiations were . . . much more than just an Anglo-American affair. They were informed by a wider political context that included a rather extensive 'North–South' dialogue that was in fact the first of its kind to shape the global financial order."[31]

These efforts at the global level were paralleled and exceeded by significant regional efforts at development and peace that took place in Asia, Africa, Latin America, and elsewhere. These efforts helped to localize and strengthen international norms such as anti-colonialism, self-determination, and non-intervention against super-power rivalry.[32] Partly due to such local contributions, the key elements of the liberal order, including capitalism, democracy, and multilateralism, have been marked by significant regional variations. One example is East Asia's relatively successful state-led capitalism, which was surely not an American invention, but may be contrasted with the laissez-faire form in the US. In East Asia, governments recognized the "limitations of markets" and sought to correct market failures with policies that promoted specific industries, directed foreign investment, and regulated financial markets.[33] To claim that such local variations are all part of a single American-led process of global ordering would be arrogant and stretching the truth.

A frontal challenge to Fukuyama's "end of history" thesis,[34] which claimed that capitalism and democracy have finally and decisively triumphed over all competing ideas, comes from a recent book by Weber and Jentleson, which argues that "the biggest, most basic questions of world politics are now open for debate."[35] Not only for debate, one might add, but also for a variety of approaches other than what America might prescribe. Consider, for example, the ideas of human development and human security. Developed by Pakistani economist Mahabub-ul Haq, they were a critique of economic liberalism (and the tendency to judge development mainly in terms of GDP growth) and the national security paradigm promoted by the US. The Grameen model of microfinance was developed by Mohammed Yunus of Bangladesh against the conventional banking practices and with the explicit rejection of assistance from the World Bank, one of the most powerful instruments of the liberal hegemonic order.

In international relations literature, there has been much debate over the effects of interdependence, institutions, and democracy, the three main pillars of a liberal international order. I am quite sympathetic to the view that these three forces have significantly positive consequences for peace.[36] But it is equally important to recognize the limitations of the liberal norms and mechanisms for peace. This leads to my fifth major point about the limits of the liberal hegemony thesis. For example, interdependence has been associated with failure to prevent conflict in the early twentieth century, as well as contributing to heightened conflict now. Under some circumstances, as Mansfield and Snyder have shown,[37] democratization can increase the danger of domestic instability and inter-state conflict, at least in the short term, as happened in the former Yugoslavia and Indonesia. Moreover, as the case of the US invasion of Iraq showed, the selective pursuit and abuse of democracy promotion by liberal powers due to their narrow strategic goals can be a trigger of conflict. Multilateral institutions are also susceptible to abuse in the hands of great powers and coalitions of weaker states. There have been numerous examples – the international intervention in Libya in 2011 being a stark one – of the manipulation of multilateral bodies, such as the UN Security Council resolutions authorizing force by the hand of the US and other Western powers to serve their narrow strategic goals.

It is also important to take note of other factors of peace that have emerged independently of the three liberal forces. Among them are nuclear weapons. Nuclear deterrence induces strategic caution and restraint and contributes to defensive security strategies by nuclear weapon states. From a realist standpoint, nuclear weapons might have been the major factor behind the peace that is claimed by liberal forces.[38] Cultural norms and identity also shape global and regional peace. While culture and identity can also be conflict-causing, one can find positive correlations due to cultural factors, arms control, and conflict management.[39] This record challenges the idea of a singular universality based on liberal politics and institutions.

To sum up, in considering the past of the liberal hegemonic order's past, it is clear that the scope of the pacific contributions of the AWO could be exaggerated, while its dark side, the degree of resistance to it, and the agency of actors other than the US, could be understated. With this backdrop, one might now turn to the question of the future of that order. Here, two questions are especially important: whether it can co-opt China and other emerging powers and whether it can continue to dominate and shape the future of multilateralism. While the issue of emerging powers will be discussed in detail in the next chapter, here I discuss briefly the case of China and the future of multilateralism.

Co-opting China

China poses the critical test of the first question. Ikenberry argues that "China has incentives and opportunities to join, while at the same time, the possibilities of it actually overturning or subverting this order are small or nonexistent."[40] That China has major stakes in the existing order is not a new argument. As Iain Johnston points out, China is today deeply engaged in the global and regional multilateral structures. Indeed, all emerging powers, including China, Japan, and India have similar orientation. But there are important differences. Consider the three major Asian powers.[41] Among these, China was the most revisionist and Japan the most conformist when it came to the prevailing world order during the cold war. India's position has been somewhat in the middle: it is best described as an adaptive, rather then revisionist or conformist posture.[42] India embraced multilateralism, such as the UN system, but not minilateralism, such as NATO-like arrangements in Asia or the Middle East. Such differences among the emerging powers are likely to continue, creating greater diversity in the future world order than that suggested by the scenario of a diffusion of the liberal hegemonic order.

But how far will China (and India) go along with the existing order? The assertion that "China will continue to actively seek to integrate into an expanded and reorganized liberal international order"[43] raises the question of what expansion and reorganization of that order would actually mean and entail. Will China simply accept the existing order without substantial changes to the norms and rules of human rights, intervention, and domestic governance? Would the US accept the changes that China seeks to carry out? The previous major shift in global power, from Britain to the US, had occurred within the framework of Western values and institutions. Even if China never becomes the leading power of the world, its rise would still fuel a desire and need for legitimizing and exporting its own values and institutions. Chinese leaders already propose ideas and institutions for domestic and international governance drawn from China's own history and culture, and seek to imagine the future world order in terms of their own past.

David Kang has outlined possible elements of a historical East Asian order in which a powerful and prosperous China would be the magnet for its neighboring countries' trade and a key source of their prosperity. He argues that, "Historically . . . When China has been strong and stable, order has been preserved. East Asian regional relations have historically been hierarchic, more peaceful, and more stable than those in the West."[44] Through a system of recognition and protection of weaker neighbors, China was a source of regional stability.[45] Kang does not claim that the classical tributary system could be revived in twenty-first-century Asia.[46] But he raises the possibility of a "hierarchical" system around China, which could provide stability in Asia given its potential as one of the most critical arenas in the world for great power rivalry in the twenty-first century.

Chinese analysts and leaders have explicitly invoked classical political ideas and inter-state systems as the basis for explaining and organizing China's approach to international relations.[47] They speak of *Tianxia* ("all under heaven"), which dates back to the Zhou dynasty[48] and implies a world order in which countries could be "harmonious but different" or achieve "harmony without uniformity."[49] One might see in this an implicit call by China to the West to leave its illiberal political system alone, while offering cooperation with it. This does not presage China's co-option into the liberal order. Drawing upon classical thinking and traditions, Chinese scholars such as Yan Xuetong also propose "new values for new international norms," such as the notion of the "Kingly way" stressing righteousness and benevolence over the more legalistic Western notions of equality and democracy. While Yan holds that these Chinese values may not always compete with, but may also complement, Western liberal norms such as justice and fairness, they "can by all means transcend the hegemonic values of the United States."[50] While these may seem propagandistic to Westerners, others are consistent with China's solidarist outlook with the developing world and this should serve as a warning signal that China, while it might accept and benefit from the current international economic structure, would be far less likely to conform to the politics and principles of the current liberal hegemonic order when organizing its own domestic politics and international political relations.

I do not believe that the emerging powers, either collectively, or China on its own, would supplant the US and assume the perch of global hegemony to the extent of the UK or the US. The limits to the global leadership role of the emerging powers will be discussed in the next chapter. A Chinese regional hegemony in Asia is unlikely to materialize. China has serious deficiencies as a global power in terms of its power projection capabilities, its ability to provide public goods, or the attraction of its ideology and values. And its myriad conflicts with neighbors – Japan,

India, Vietnam, or the Philippines – would hold it down from achieving both regional and global hegemony. But not being able to challenge American power frontally does not mean accepting American values and leadership. China can surely help thwart the preservation of the US liberal hegemony.

What about other emerging powers? The chances of their being co-opted into a liberal hegemonic order without that order undergoing fundamental changes are slim. This observation applies not only to Russia, but also to other emerging democratic powers such as India and Brazil. The case of Brazil, argues Brazilian scholar Marcus Tourinho, refutes the view that weaker states have embraced postwar US hegemony "for the benefits of an 'open,' user friendly liberal international order." In his view, "While in fact the aspects of contemporary international order that Ikenberry calls 'liberal' (institutions, rule of law, etc.) are essentially welcomed by Brazil, the country has at the same time consistently rejected and resisted the hegemonic practices that so often have accompanied it."[51]

Some argue that the emerging powers agree with the core elements of the current liberal order, such as cooperative security, international institutions, shared sovereignty, and democratic community, but "oppose the implicit and explicit hierarchies of international institutions and the many privileges often enjoyed by great powers in international deliberations."[52] Apart from the difficulty in identifying some of these elements as exclusively liberal rather than universal principles, their support for shared sovereignty and democratic community can be overstated, especially if the latter connotes the idea of an "alliance of democracies" or "league of democracies" that some proponents of liberal order, with the implicit support of the Obama administration, have proposed.[53] Moreover, how does one go about creating such an alliance? Expanding NATO would be the least likely path. It would be highly controversial and certain to be rejected by several democracies, including India and Indonesia, in a repeat of their rejection of the invitation to join SEATO in 1954. An informal network is more plausible, but labeling it as an "alliance" or "league" would be just as controversial with the same countries. The degree of ideological affinity and the shared perceptions of security among the members of such an alliance are insufficient to make it viable. None of the emerging powers share the US approach to democracy promotion. In the case of Brazil, these differences were pronounced in 2002, when Brazil supported the reinstatement of Venezuela's Hugo Chavez after he had been ousted in a coup, while the US had promptly recognized the government installed by the coup.

Moreover, it could be dangerously counterproductive. China is sure to see this as part of a containment strategy, especially now that the US is pivoting to Asia militarily. The alliance or democracies and the pivot (which relies on the network of America's treaty allies and partners in Asia) would thus overlap, feeding Beijing's paranoia. How this might be a positive force for peace and security in Asia and the world is hard to see. Instead, it might fuel Chinese insecurity and assertiveness.

"It is illusory," argues Kupchan, "to presume that a country's form of government will be such an important determinant of its geopolitical alignment; democracies are simply not destined to ally with each other as a matter of course."[54] In this context, the problems facing the idea of a regional alliance of democracies in Asia, involving the US, Japan, Australia, and India, which has been mooted since 2006, are worth noting. Even as democracies, the political and social systems of the four differ from each other. India's level of economic development is markedly lower than those of the other three. And developing a shared vision of world order will be difficult. Although India no longer champions non-alignment, it remains wary of any alliances – formal or informal – with Western powers. Unlike Australia and Japan, India refused to join the "coalition of the willing" formed by the Bush

administration when it invaded Iraq. India has opposed
the US policy of isolating Iran, even as New Delhi does
not endorse Iran's nuclear ambitions.

It is a fallacy to assume that just because China, India,
and other rising powers have benefitted from the liberal
hegemonic order, they would abide by its norms and institutions. They may not seek to overthrow it but push for
changes that might significantly alter the rules and institutions of that order. Kupchan is especially skeptical that the
rising powers will follow the Western path to modernity.
Referring to the unique conditions that produced capitalism, constitutional rule, and democracy in the West, such
as the disintegration of feudalism, urbanization, and the
rise of a commercial class to challenge the dominance of
the Church, monarchy, and aristocracy, Kupchan argues,
"today's rising powers are each following unique paths
toward modernity based on their own political, demo-
graphic, topographic, and socioeconomic conditions.
Accordingly, they are developing versions of modernity
divergent from the West's." Combined with cultural
factors, this would push the rising states to "follow their
own developmental paths and embrace their own views
about domestic governance and how best to organize the
international system of the twenty-first century."[55]

American Power and the Future of Multilateralism

The believers in the liberal hegemonic order, and here one
would include the Obama administration, seek to distin-
guish between power and leadership. To them, multilateral
cooperation through international organization is the key
means of ensuring the liberal order's continued legitimacy
and America's pre-eminent role in global affairs. As Hillary
Clinton put it at her confirmation hearing as Secretary of
State in 2009:

So let me say it clearly: the United States can, must, and will lead in this new century . . . The world looks to us because America has the reach and resolve to mobilize the shared effort needed to solve problems on a global scale – in defense of our own interests, but also as a force for progress. In this we have no rival.

This notwithstanding, America's commitment to multilateralism has been both selective and self-serving. The most obvious example of this was the rampant unilateralism of the George W. Bush administration. While the Obama administration has made more noises about going multilateral, it has not ended the US opposition to the International Criminal Court (ICC). In 2002, the US had threatened to veto all UN peacekeeping missions unless it was granted a blanket immunity from the ICC. While the Obama administration has relaxed the US opposition to the ICC, it still demands that all ICC investigations should be decided with the approval of the UN Security Council, where it can wield the veto. Critics consider this policy as a threat to "the Court's legitimacy as an independent institution."[56] The Obama administration theoretically supports UN Security Council reform "that enhances the UN's overall performance, effectiveness and efficiency to meet the challenges of the new century."[57] But it has not provided leadership toward this goal. A key element of UN reform is the reform of veto. The US has been the main user of the veto, one of the key targets of UN reform proposals. Between 1986 and 1995, the US exercised veto 24 times, compared to 2 for the USSR/ Russia, 8 for Britain, 3 for France, and zero for China. Between 1996 and 2012, the US has exercised veto 13 times, compared to 7 times for Russia, and 7 times for China. (Additionally, 43 vetoes have been used to block nominees for Secretary General, although these vetoes were cast during closed sessions of the council).[58] A package of reform measures for the IMF, adopted in 2010 with much fanfare to give more share of the decision-making to the emerging countries, has stalled because the US Congress has yet to ratify it. These measures would shift six percentage points of the IMF quota share to the emerging markets, move two of the 24 IMF executive board seats from Europe to developing countries, and introduce elections for all seats in the IMF's executive board (which under the current system are appointed by the five largest members). The delay in ratifying the measures by the stipulated deadline of September 2012 that "damaged US credibility, also damaged the credibility of the Fund and the G20."[59]

In considering these challenges to multilateralism, one has to keep in mind that the very conceptualization of multilateralism is American-centric. John Ruggie's influential 1993 edited volume, *Multilateralism Matters*, embodies this view. Ruggie concedes that multilateralism was not a post-war American invention. Yet, "Looking more closely at the post-World War II situation . . . it was less the fact of American *hegemony* that accounts for the explosion of multilateral arrangements than of *American* hegemony."[60] Ruggie contrasts post-war American-led multilateralism with the New Economic Order of Nazi Germany. That order, though it coordinated economic relations among more than three states, would not qualify as multilateral because it was founded upon a system of bilateralist trade and clearing arrangements between Germany and foreign trading partners that made the system "inherently and fundamentally discriminatory."[61] The Nazi order functioned as a sphere of influence, lacking in openness and equal access, even though Germany did often import more from its partners than it exported to them.

This conceptualization of multilateralism has been thoroughly embraced and supplemented by the AWO. In a previous book, Ikenberry agreed that multilateralism went hand in hand with American hegemony. His explanation for the pursuit of multilateralism by the US is that, through multilateral institutions, a hegemon like the US extracts loyalty and compliance from the weaker states by promising not to threaten them or "exercise [its] power arbitrarily."[62]

One should not forget, however, that in the above narrative, it is the US that crafts the institutional framework of multilateralism. The weaker states merely "accept the deal,"[63] mainly to mitigate their fear of domination or abandonment by the US.[64] Despite the promise of being spared exploitation and domination,[65] what is the situation in the event of their non-compliance with America's wishes? Institutions created by hegemonic power, including the US, are always pregnant with the possibility of exercising coercive means. And such institutions may not always be viewed as legitimate or benign by the weaker states because they fundamentally represent an unequal relationship and a form of dominance. For example, the so-called multilateral security systems created by the United States in the third world, such as SEATO and the Central Treaty Organization (CENTO), were criticized and rejected by a number of countries, including India and Indonesia.[66]

Instead of joining with a hegemonic power, weaker states may develop cooperative institutions to keep all the great powers out of their affairs. During the cold war, many nationalist leaders from the developing world rejected US-inspired security and economic pacts which conflicted with their desire for autonomy and equality. One example is a regional multilateral grouping of small and weak states, the Association of Southeast Asian Nations (ASEAN), which developed a framework for limiting the role of all outside powers, including the US, as the US intervention in Vietnam seemed to them increasingly fruitless and counterproductive. The lesson here is that weaker states may develop regional multilateral institutions that differ from a globally hegemonic order and are more suited to their own specific goals and identities. Such institutions may either exclude stronger powers or socialize them on their own terms and on the basis of locally developed norms, as opposed to principles and modalities laid down by the hegemonic power. One finds examples in Latin America's opposition to the US Monroe doctrine, and ASEAN's Zone of Peace, Freedom and Neutrality (ZOFPAN) during the cold war. Stronger powers, unable to secure local legitimacy for institutions proposed by themselves, may well accept cooperation proposed and developed by weaker states even when such institutions constrain their options and behavior. It is impossible to understand the origin and growth of multilateral institutions in Asia today – especially ASEAN and the ASEAN Regional Forum (ARF) and the East Asia Summit – without taking into consideration such possibilities for a form of multilateralism that is not dictated or led by a great power.

The problems with the American-centric conception of multilateralism are fourfold. First, it was, at least initially, quite state-centric. The place and role of civil society or non-state actors, which would present a powerful challenge to the state-centric conceptualization of multilateralism, were ignored in this conceptualization. Second, it stresses the benign aspect of the role of international institutions created by the US within the framework of the liberal hegemonic order, and ignores their negative and coercive role. It assumes that the principles and mechanisms of cooperation which have contributed to common interests in the West have an equally benign and beneficial effect in the third world. Yet these institutions have also exercised a coercive role, such as the IMF's "structural adjustment" policy in Africa in the 1980s. As Keeley argues, "Liberal approaches assume, rather than establish, regimes as benevolent, voluntary, cooperative and legitimate."[67] International institutions often reflect and preserve hegemony. They "universalise the norms proper to a structure of world power, and that structure of power maintains itself through support of these institutions. In that sense, institutions are ballasts to the status quo."[68]

Third, the American-centric practice of multilateralism has inspired theoretical approaches that pay little attention to the multilateralism of the non-Western, developing world.[69] Regime theory, a key element of the liberal understanding of multilateralism, was initially mostly concerned with relationships among the Northern countries. As Robert Cox notes:

> regime theory has much to say about economic cooperation among the Group of 7 (G-7) and other groupings of advanced capitalist countries with regard to problems common to them. It has correspondingly less to say about attempts to change the structure of world economy, e.g. in the Third World demand for a New International Economic Order (NIEO). Indeed, regimes are designed to stabilize the world economy and have the effect . . . of inhibiting and deterring states from initiating radical departures from economic orthodoxy.[70]

Fourth, the American-centric liberal conception of multilateralism has ignored the role of regional multilateralism. Multilateralism is not an exclusively global phenomenon. Regional organizations can be multilateral because they too may abide by the principles of indivisibility and reciprocity. In other words, regionalism and multilateralism (or universalism) need not be mutually competitive and exclusive, as some liberal pundits argue.[71] Yet it is revealing that the influential work *Multilateralism Matters* contained chapters only on NATO, the European Community, and the Conference on Security and Cooperation in Europe (CSCE), as examples of such region-specific multilateralism. It left out all other parts of the world.[72]

If one accepts that the United States intrinsically favored a multilateral approach, why did it not encourage multilateralism in Asia or other regions of the world? Asia is of particular significance here, both then and now, since it was a key theater of the cold war, a region of great economic dynamism, and, in the views of many, the arena of the most significant geopolitical competition of the twenty-first century, between the US and China. Surely, the absence of NATO in Asia would challenge the close association between multilateralism and US hegemony? One answer to this puzzle could be that the power asymmetries between the United States and its putative multilateral partners were so large that a multilateral approach would have amounted to free-riding on the part of the allies without significantly adding to the US strategic capacity to meet the Soviet and Chinese threats.[73] But Christopher Hemmer and Peter Katzenstein have argued that racism and prejudice also played a part. For them, genuine multilateralism requires a measure of collective identification among partners. While post-war US strategic planners identified with their European partners who "could be trusted with the additional power a multilateral institution would give them," they "did not believe that the Southeast Asian states could be trusted with the increased influence a multilateral institution would offer, nor was there any sense that these states deserved such a multilateral structure."[74] Another explanation is that the US under the Eisenhower administration wanted but could not establish a viable multilateral security framework in Asia, due to opposition from a group of Asian leaders to the particular form of multilateralism that the US sought to impose. This was an anti-communist alliance called SEATO, which the leaders of India, Indonesia, Burma, and others perceived as a form of neo-colonial domination.[75] While these explanations differ, together they suggest no natural or inevitable association between multilateralism and US hegemony.

In recent times, the American-centric conception of multilateralism has come under challenge. For example, the idea of "new multilateralism"[76] offers a broader conception of multilateralism, acknowledging the role of social movements, rather than just of states. It also takes into account principles of multilateral cooperation that are "post-hegemonic" in the sense that they are not beholden to US power and purpose. In the security domain, they feature the notion of common and cooperative security (an European idea) rather than national security (an American idea), or the principle of "security with" that underpins the Organization for Security and Cooperation in Europe (OSCE) and ASEAN, rather than "security against," which was the foundational principle of NATO. In the economic domain, instead of the traditional liberal focus on free trade and market-led development promoted by the US and US-backed institutions like the IMF, WTO, and the World Bank, the new multilateralism acknowledges "alternative methods of social organizing and cultural diversity,"[77] including an emphasis on equality, social justice, and the distribution of wealth.

The traditional notion of multilateralism privileges not only the role of US power, but also the role of Western transnational activists. It does so often at the expense of regional or local advocates in the non-Western world. For example, the dominant model of transnational human rights advocacy, the "boomerang," has been criticized for obscuring "local embodiments of human rights norms in the developing world."[78] The "location, obscure language, and marginality" of local human rights groups results in limited attention to their role by transnational human rights groups.[79] Yet these groups often play a critical role in the promotion of human rights. As James Ron observes, "Transnational NGOs and networks can monitor, inform, and advocate all they want, but without serious investments of time and effort by local human rights champions, nothing much will change on the ground."[80]

Finally, to be viable and legitimate, multilateralism must be inclusive in its scope and purpose. Returning to the idea of an alliance of democracies as a form of liberal multilateralism, it may be wiser to seek a wider multilateral framework such as the Inter-American Democratic Charter of the OAS, or the Bali Democracy Forum launched by Indonesia, rather than pursue the idea of an alliance of democracies that might damage relations with China, and may not garner enough unity of purpose among the allies to be viable or meaningful enough to sustain the idea of a reformed or reconstituted American-led liberal hegemonic order.

– 4 –

Emerging Powers

The Hype of the Rest?

The terms "emerging powers" and "rising powers" recognize the growing economic as well as political and strategic status of a group of nations, most if not all of which were once categorized (and in some accounts still are) as part of the "third world" or "global South." The definition of who belongs in these categories is neither fixed nor uncontroversial. These terms are often used to include countries such as the BRICS (Brazil, Russia, India, China, and South Africa), as well as Indonesia, Mexico, Argentina, Australia, Saudi Arabia, South Korea, and Turkey. Andrew Cooper has observed that "the depiction of rising powers" has been "expansive, fluid, and contested . . . No one acronym has the field to itself."[1] The same can be said of the term "emerging powers." For example, despite its seeming conflation with "emerging powers," the term "rising powers" is normally associated with countries that have a clear potential to become great powers, such as China, India, and Brazil. The term "emerging powers" indicates countries such as Indonesia, South Korea, Mexico, Nigeria, and South Africa, which are not perceived to be headed for international great power status. (For convenience, I will use the term "emerging powers," a broader category which subsumes "rising powers.") Russia is an odd presence in the ranks of the rising/emerging powers category, since it is really a traditional European great power, which was also a military superpower during the cold war. Some analysts even see it, at least in terms of its geopolitical behavior, as an "outdated great power."[2] Another term that complicates the picture is that of "regional powers," a category that relies more on physical and material attributes of a country relative to its immediate neighbors. Not all emerging powers are counted as regional powers, though. For example, should South Korea and Argentina, while recognized as emerging powers, be counted as regional powers? These uncertain and contested categorizations are important, as they affect the discussion of their role in the world governance and order.

The popularity of the idea of emerging powers had much to do with the term "BRIC" – Brazil, Russia, India, China. This was a term coined by a Goldman Sachs analyst in 2001 in the context, it must not be forgotten, not of describing their power in global order, but in describing the potential of the "emerging market economies" in relation to their investors in 2001.[3] South Africa joined the group in 2010, thus making it "BRICS." In a 2010 report, Goldman Sachs defended the concept by pointing out that over the preceding 10 years BRIC had contributed over a third of world GDP growth and had grown from a sixth of the world economy to almost a quarter (in PPP terms). Its projections envisaged the BRICS, as an aggregate, overtaking the US by 2018.[4]

The Goldman Sachs analyst, Jim O'Neill, is now less bullish about the economic prospects of the BRICS. But the fashion show continues with new acronyms such as CIVETS (Colombia, Indonesia, Vietnam, Egypt, Turkey, and South Africa), "breakout nations"[5] (Turkey, the Philippines, Thailand, India, Poland, Colombia, South Korea, and Nigeria). Another one is MIST (Mexico, Indonesia, South Korea, and Turkey). How much of this is a self-promoting marketing ploy by business consulting firms is a moot question.

To some extent, recognition as an emerging/rising power is decided by membership in clubs, the most well known of which is the BRICS. But there are other club designations, some of them largely notional, such as BRIICS (including Indonesia), BASIC (BRIC minus Russia, but with South Africa), while others are functioning, such as IBSA (India, Brazil, South Africa), BRICSAM (add South Africa and Mexico). At a broader level, the key point of reference is the G-20,[6] a club known for its importance in global finance, membership in which almost automatically earns a country the label of "emerging power." Even in economic terms, the category of emerging powers is not homogeneous. This is true even of the relatively compact group of the BRICS (now with the addition of South Africa), as table 4.1 shows.

For the most part, membership is based on traditional indices of power, or on material capabilities, primarily economic but also military, as well as the relative size and population of nations. Each BRICS member is a significant military power, especially relative to its own neighbors. Membership in these clubs does not necessarily recognize soft power, or leadership in ideas, innovation, and problem-solving, or what might be called intellectual and entrepreneurial leadership. This leaves out a few countries known for their global and regional leadership role, past and present, and raises questions about how meaningful the term "emerging power" is, as a new force in world politics. For example, Singapore is left out of these emerging power clubs, yet it is an enterprising nation when it comes to Asian and global economic cooperation. Angry at its exclusion from the G-20, Singapore helped to found a global governance group at the UN. Costa Rica under Oscar Arias was a key player in resolving the Central American conflict in the 1980s. Thailand founded ASEAN, one of the most successful regional groupings in the developing world. Despite its initial economic focus, the G-20

Table 4.1 Overview of BRICS: 1990 and 2010

Country	Rank in world	GDP (PPP bn)	GDP ($ bn)		Share in world GDP (%)		Per capita GDP ($)	
			1990	2010	1990	2010	1990	2010
Brazil	8	2,172	508	2,090	3.3	2.9	3,464	10,816
Russia	6	2,223	–	1,465	–	3	–	10,437
India	4	4,060	326	1,538	3.1	5.4	378	1,265
China	2	10,086	390	5,878	3.9	13.6	341	4,382
South Africa	26	524	112	357	0.9	0.7	5,456	7,158

Source: Suresh Singh and Memory Dube, "BRICS and World Order: A Beginner's Guide" (<http://cuts-international.org/BRICS-TERN/pdf/BRICS_and_the_World_Order-A_Beginners_Guide.pdf>). Reprinted with permission

Table 4.2 Economies of G20 members (2009 estimated)

Member	GDP (nominal PPP) $ USD	GDP (per capita PPP) $ USD	Population
South Africa	$505.3 billion	$10,300	49,052,489
Canada	$1.279 trillion	$38,200	33,487,208
US	$14.14 trillion	$46,000	307,212,123
Mexico	$1.465 trillion	$13,200	111,211,789
Argentina	$548.8 billion	$13,400	40,913,584
Brazil	$2.013 trillion	$10,100	198,739,269
China	$8.748 trillion	$6,600	1,338,612,968
Japan	$4.15 trillion	$32,700	127,078,679
South Korea	$1.364 trillion	$28,100	48,508,972
India	$3.57 trillion	$3,100	1,156,897,766
Indonesia	$962.5 billion	$4,000	240,271,522
Saudi Arabia	$592.3 billion	$20,600	28,686,633
Russia	$2.11 trillion	$15,100	140,041,247
Turkey	$874.5 billion	$11,400	76,805,524
Australia	$851.1 billion	$40,000	21,262,641
France	$2.097 trillion	$32,600	64,420,073
Germany	$2.81 trillion	$34,100	82,329,758
Italy	$1.739 trillion	$29,900	58,126,212
UK	$2.128 trillion	$34,800	61,113,205
EU	$14.43 trillion	$32,500	492,387,344

Source: CIA World Factbook Data

has aspirations to manage security issues. Yet some of the most important security actors of the developing world, such as Egypt and Nigeria, are not part of it.

Despite these problems, the term "emerging powers" has secured for itself a prominent place in the discussion of the developing world order. But while there is a good deal of noise about the emerging powers, mostly created by the powers themselves, the analysis of their role has been shaped by a narrow and short-term policy focus, much of it having to do with the global economic crisis since 2008. There is less accounting of the gap between their aspirations and capabilities, on the one hand, and between the benefits they bring into and the burdens they impose on "global governance" and order, on the other hand.

The G-20: Promise and Performance

There are two main candidates vying for the status of being the most important member of the new global power elite, the BRICS and the G-20. Although the BRIC idea goes back to 1990, and the G-20 was established in 1999, a turning point in their role in global reordering came with the outbreak of the global financial crisis in 2008. The crisis led this select group of states not only to play a major role in fashioning the global response to the crisis, but also created opportunities for them to shape the debate over the future of global governance and world order.

However, this has not been a smooth sailing. BRICS has the advantage of being a small and compact group. But economic disparities (already mentioned) aside, its members are also divided in terms of their domestic political systems – between democratic Brazil, India, and South Africa on the one hand, and China's communist regime and Russia's authoritarian turn on the other. One consequence of this is that the BRICS group is open to criticism for ignoring democratic issues even as they demand greater democratization of international relations. For example, by joining the BRICS, South Africa was seen as placing power and self-interest over principles that it had espoused as a member of IBSA, with India and Brazil, including a commitment to human rights and democracy not shared by BRICS members China and Russia. Three of the BRICS members – Russia, China, and India – are nuclear weapon states while South Africa and Brazil are not, the latter having renounced nuclear weapons earlier. Hence attitudes toward nuclear non-proliferation within the BRICS are not convergent.

More importantly, the BRICS countries do not seem to have enough cement to hold them together on the key issue of global reordering. A key example is the competitive relationship between China and India. And the discordant voices within the grouping about issues of global order, ranging from climate change to UN Security Council reform (especially between India and China), has not helped the group to project an image of coherence and credibility. Commenting on intra-BRICS differences, a Chinese analyst asks, "Why does it put Brazil, Russia, India, and China together and coin a new word? These four countries are actually quite different from each other in many ways and even in fundamental nature."[7] Thus, these differences do undermine their collective clout in international affairs. It is a fair question whether, despite the hype surrounding it, membership in the BRICS is more of a status symbol (and a way of attracting attention from foreign investors) than a means to real decision-making authority in global affairs.[8]

The G-20 is perhaps a more credible agent for reshaping global governance. This group represents 80 percent of the world's population, 90 percent of the world's GDP, 90 percent of the world's finance, and 80 percent of the world's trade. It is credited with "implementing the largest coordinated macroeconomic stimulus in history, which has successfully arrested a potentially deep global recession."[9] Largely because of its success in arresting the financial crisis, this institution has described itself (at its Pittsburg Summit in September 2009) as the "world's premier forum for international economic cooperation."[10] The former EU foreign policy chief, Javier Solana, calls it the "only force in which world powers and the emerging countries sit as equals at the same table."[11] Others see it as having the "potential to alter the international order almost by stealth."[12]

Supporters of the G-20 see many benefits coming from its role in global governance. Bruce Jones argues that it can make the UN more effective by bridging the gap between the governing mechanisms of the secretariat and those of the specialized agencies, like the IMF and World

Bank. It can also make coordination between the UN's security and economic groupings, for example, the Security Council and ECOSOC, easier. This might help with the prospects for the management and resolution of regional conflicts like those in the Middle East and Asia. It can stimulate discussion and debate over global issues, and get other multilateral bodies to act faster and better "extract excellence" from them.[13]

A key part of the agenda of the G-20 includes reform of global institutions. Here the emerging powers are on solid ground. The major global institutions – the UN, IMF, and World Bank, etc., – were created in the aftermath of World War II and reflected the capabilities and influence of nations in that era. That their future effectiveness and legitimacy depends on adapting to the new realities of the twenty-first century cannot be seriously questioned.

The G-20 has the potential to advance the reform of global governance. It certainly gave a new lease of life to debate over reform of global institutions like the IMF and the World Bank, including the initial step taken in 2010 by IMF members to adjust its members' voting quotas marginally in favor of the developing countries (which places Brazil, China, India, and Russia among the 10 top shareholders of the IMF),[14] and move toward a fully democratically elected executive board.

But, overall, the G-20 has made little headway on the reform of global institutions. The political and practical obstacles to making global institutions more democratic and inclusive are huge. Expanding and reforming the UN Security Council, especially its veto system, has proven to be virtually impossible. The actual changes induced by the G-20 in the global governance system are still marginal. The reason for this is not just resistance from the West, although this is a factor. It has also to do with disunity within the ranks of the G-20, and not just between India and China or China and Japan. For example, the immediate regional rivals of Nigeria, Brazil, and India have vigorously opposed other countries' quest for a permanent seat in the UN Security Council. "Egypt and South Africa wonder about Nigeria's special qualifications, while Argentina and Mexico, Indonesia and Pakistan question the choice of Brazil and India. Smaller countries, in turn, are unhappy about any system that will strengthen the powerful at their expense."[15] Another recent example is the failure of the G-20 to put up a common candidate from the ranks of the developing countries, and Brazil's refusal to back up a Mexican candidate, which might have helped keep the position of the IMF chief in the hands of the French as Christine Lagarde replaced Dominique Strauss-Kahn.[16]

Moreover, questions remain as to the effectiveness and legitimacy of the G-20 in the whole new architecture of global order. Despite the credit it receives for its role in managing the 2008 global financial crisis, the group's contribution to the long-term health of the global economic system remains questionable. As Malaysian economist Mahani Zainal Abidin argued, the G-20 has not effectively addressed "fundamental issues – such as the global imbalances, exchange rate alignment, preventing bubbles, and discouraging excessive risk taking."[17] There are also questions and uncertainties concerning its institutionalization (it still lacks a secretariat). Its credibility has been marred by a lack of continuity from one summit to the next. It is also not clear whether the G-20 would replace the G-8. As Solana put it, "holding a G-8 summit just before a G-20 summit . . . simply serves to prolong the maintenance of separate clubs, which is unsustainable."[18] Europe is over-represented in the G-20. And countries which should have been in the G-20 are not there. The issue of representation might be addressed through "smart inclusion,"[19] including the more universal organizations like the Development Committee of the World Bank, or the IMF's International Monetary and Financial Committee, as well as other regional groupings and organizations such as ASEAN and the African Union. The EU is already included. But the move toward inclusiveness is likely to be controversial.

To date, there is no consensus on whether the G-20 should remain a "crisis committee" (the role played in addressing the 2008 crisis) to deal with financial volatility, or become a more regularized "steering committee" to manage a wider set of issues on a more regular basis. Some view it as a "global focus group" that draws attention to major global concerns. It has been criticized for a "disciplinary, coercive culture" and offers little "evidence of . . . being a substitute for U.S. hegemonic control."[20] The G-20 has also struggled with agenda expansion beyond finance to include development (e.g., the Seoul Development Consensus adopted at the Seoul Summit in 2010), environment (green growth at the Los Cabos summit in 2012), and security issues. The comparative advantage of the G-20 over other institutions, such as the World Bank, UNSC, and the Rio+20, is still unproven. Taking on too many issues can backfire and compromise its credibility, as happened under the French presidency at Cannes in 2011, with the anti-corruption initiative, food security and financial transaction tax, and so on. In the meantime, the Eurozone crisis has affected its standing negatively, overshadowed by the European Central Bank and the IMF.

The emergence of the G-20 group has larger implications for global order. It has been viewed as the beginning of the end of a structure of global governance dominated by the Western nations and international institutions controlled by them. The G-20 has the potential to blur or bridge the traditional North–South, or West versus the Rest, faultline in world order. For example, on the issue of the IMF governance reform, the US (at least the Obama administration) was aligned with China, India, and Brazil in supporting increased representation of the emerging powers, against Europe, which was resisting any reduction in the number of the European seats.

Are we then witnessing a new spirit of partnership and cooperation between the North and the South, replacing the old mistrust and rivalry? One should be reminded that some of the recent examples of North–South cooperation, whether undertaken by the G-20 or not, are crisis-induced. Such examples, aside from the 2008 financial crisis, might include 9/11, Somali pirates, and Libya – although in Libya's case the faultlines re-emerged once it became clear that the Anglo-French intervention exceeded the UN Security Council mandate as understood not only by China and Russia but also by South Africa and Brazil. Whether crisis-driven responses will endure in building long-term cooperation, and add up to something more permanent, extending to the more traditional security dilemmas – such as that between the US and China, China and Japan, China and India, and Russia and West Europe – remains to be seen.

Power South and the Poor South

There is another important question concerning whether, in bridging the traditional North–South divide at the elite level, the new cooperation might create a new division: between the Power South and the Poor South. Here, some historical background may be of interest. The G-20 has a lineage with the historic Asia-Africa Conference held in Bandung, Indonesia, in 1955. Among the G-20 members, six attended that conference: China (People's Republic), India, Indonesia, Japan, Turkey, and Saudi Arabia. From South Africa, then under apartheid, two members of the African National Congress attended as observers. The most conspicuous omission in the G-20 of a Bandung attendee is that of Egypt.

The Bandung conference was influenced by the cold war divisions. Turkey (backed by Thailand and the Philippines) clashed with India (backed by Indonesia and communist China). And two of the G-20 members, the UK and the USA, did their very best to sabotage the conference. The UK worried that Bandung might lead to increased pressure to relinquish its still considerable colonial possessions in Asia and elsewhere. The US feared a propaganda coup by communist China. Acting in concert, the two powers prevented Ghana's Nkrumah from attending Bandung and lobbied and pressured their allies among the Bandung invitees to frustrate not only communist China, but also the "neutralists" like India, Indonesia, and Burma, who were essentially running the show. They even supplied propaganda material (background papers) telling allied nations like Turkey, Thailand, and the Philippines what to say and what do at the conference. Australia made it known that it did not want to be invited to Bandung. Canada was watchful and wary. The Soviet Union overtly supported Bandung but was nervous about China getting too close to Asia with the risk of diluting the Sino-Soviet Bloc (although it did break up soon thereafter, and Bandung might have been one of the reasons). The Bandung conference laid the foundation of the political solidarity of the third world. The latter became a powerful symbol of the global North–South divide.[21]

Fast forward to the present: just as Bandung was the most talked-about development in the third world in the late 1950s, the most talked-about group featuring in the South today is the G-20. But there are key differences, some with positive implications for the South, others less so.

First, several among the Bandung alumni of the G-20 have themselves changed drastically. South Africa is no longer ruled by the apartheid regime. For Japan, Bandung was the first foray into international diplomacy after defeat in World War II. It has emerged as a key player in Asia and the world. Bandung was communist China's debut on the world diplomatic stage. A poor and fledgling communist country, China then easily invited mistrust. India's Jawaharlal Nehru did his very best (at the cost of his own image and India's influence) to project China as more Asian than communist, partly to wean it away from the Soviet Union. China is now the world's pre-eminent emerging power with a vital role in the global governance architecture. India no longer professes Nehruvian idealism and has gone well past its policy of non-alignment. It no longer wants to unify Asia; that task has long been ceded to ASEAN. Turkey and Indonesia have become more democratic. Indonesia has made a painful but unmistakable transition to democracy, whereas at the time of the Bandung conference it was sliding into authoritarianism. The South is no longer led by the likes of ideological heavyweights: Nehru, Nasser, Nkrumah, or Mao (represented by the more moderate Zhou Enlai), but by technocrats like India's Manmohan Singh and China's former leader, Hu Jintao. The transition from the firebrand Sukarno to the introverted Susilo Banbang Yudhoyono signifies this shift.

These changes in the South are important factors in shaping the politics of the G-20 and attest to its potential to bridge the North–South divide. Bandung was exclusively a South–South event whereas the G-20 is a North–South forum. Bandung's focus was political, whereas the G-20 is, and is likely to remain, primarily an economic forum, even if it incorporates some political-strategic role.

At the same time, some old North–South divisions remain, and there are now new issues, such as the carbon emission reduction targets and creating a new architecture of financial governance that did not exist in 1955. Key members of the G-20, particularly India and China, stake out positions that are still framed in their predicament and perspective as members of the South. For them, national development goals take priority over complying with the West's demands for greener standards.

It is tempting to view the G-20 as the end of the South and a foundation for global North–South cooperation. But it may also spell the beginnings of a new polarization in international relations. The Bandung conference and its offshoot, the Non-Aligned Movement, were broad and inclusive groupings insofar as the South was concerned. The G-20 is plagued with questions about its level of representation and legitimacy. While some members, such as India, Indonesia, South Africa, Brazil, and China, claim to speak for the South within the G-20, the G-20 itself is seen as an "exclusive club" that further marginalizes the interests and voices of the poorest nations. As one observer points out, "the world's poorest nations are increasingly recognizing that these newly emergent industrial and oil powers no longer speak for them. The international press has also blurred the distinction between developing and emerging economies, making little mention that the G20 nations have become part of the global financial oligarchy in recent years."[22] The G-20 members who are from the South seem keen to leave the rather pejorative label of "third world" behind. They aspire to be leaders of the world, not just of the South. Nations represented at Bandung, including Nehru's India, Mao's China, and Nasser's Egypt, harbored no illusions about achieving global great power status, whether individually or collectively. But today, China, India, Brazil, and Japan all aspire to be global great powers.

The Bandung conference was marred by an open display of differences between the neutralists such as India, Indonesia, Burma, and Ceylon, on the one hand, and the pro-Western camp led by Turkey, Pakistan, Thailand, and the Philippines, on the other hand. There was also the perception at Bandung, albeit exaggerated by Western media, of serious Sino–Indian competition. Today the rivalry between China and India is perceived as more serious and there is additional competition between China and Japan, which was in no position to compete at Bandung. There is the likelihood that competition among the G-20 members could spill over into other parts of the South, like the Sino–Indian competition over African resources and markets, or competition among Russia, China, and Brazil over arms sales to African countries.

The G-20 may also weaken third world regionalism, which has been a building bloc for South–South cooperation. Several members of the G-20, India and China included, do not enjoy the status of spokesperson for their respective regions or sub-regions, and may have less incentive to do so now they have acquired seats on the G-20 table. Unlike South Africa, which claims to consult with the Africa Union on its G-20 role as the sole African member of the grouping, none of the Asian countries are known to consult with their neighbors in shaping the agenda of the G-20. Indonesia, which established considerable regional legitimacy through ASEAN, is now indicating a desire to overstep ASEAN and focus on its G-20 role. In the case of Brazil, a key question is whether its foreign policy should "be focused on improved trading relationships within South America so as to strengthen MERCOSUR, or should Brazil assert its leadership of the G-20 and use that position to 'reshape the economic order as well as international politics' [as its then president, Lula, put it in New Delhi in June 2007] with a more global projection of its interests?"[23] This will not be an easy dilemma to resolve, either for Brazil or the other G-20 nations, especially when regional support is important in fulfilling their global leadership aspirations.

Norm-taking and Norm-making

In the traditional view of norms in international relations, the developing or third world nations are usually seen as norm-takers, rather than as norm-makers. But the third world countries have not just been passive recipients of international norms.[24] They have also been active in reinterpreting and giving a more expansive meaning to some of the traditional norms, such as non-intervention and equality of states. Their role has also involved creating new norms for the developing world (or the third world). One leading example here would be the norms of the non-aligned movement, which called for the third world nations to abstain from participation in cold war military alliances led by any of the two superpowers. In recent years, they have also contributed to the development of such norms as "common but differentiated responsibility" in building a global climate change regime. This norm implies that, while both the North and the South have a common stake in protecting the environment, the North bears the primary responsibility for the global environmental crisis and thus should bear a larger part of the costs of environmental protection, including through transfer of resources and technology to the South so that the latter can reduce its dependence on technologies damaging to the environment.[25] Moreover, a good deal of their normative role has occurred at the regional level, where institutions have developed distinctive rules and processes of conflict management and cooperation-building.[26]

Some argue that the emerging powers identify with values "favoring equity and justice for the less powerful and seeking curtailment of unilateral or plurilateral or coalitional activity by the most powerful."[27] It is also clear that the emerging powers remain wedded to the traditional norms of international relations, especially sovereignty and non-intervention, rather than newer principles, such as the Responsibility to Protect (R2P). Hurrell, however, has warned that the emerging power might reinforce some of the bad norms of international relations, including the dangers of economic nationalism and "resource mercantilism."[28]

When it comes to global norms, the emerging powers display divergent attitudes, reflecting domestic political conditions and security policies. Part of the reason for their staunch support for non-intervention has to do with the fact that many emerging powers have significant internal conflicts. To mention a few, India's include the Maoist insurgency afflicting its eastern and central provinces (states), and older ongoing conflicts in Northeast India and Kashmir. China's internal challenges include conflicts in Tibet and Xinjiang, and the threat of political unrest, inspired by economic grievances, corruption scandals, and demand for political space against a totalitarian regime. Russia not only has ongoing conflicts in Chechnya, but also has the problem of the "hyper-centralization and personalization of the political system," as well as "corruption, rent addiction and the dysfunctional relationship between the centre and the Russian regions." South Africa's challenge is the potential for acute social conflict inspired by the greatest incidence of inequality in the world.[29]

When it comes to non-intervention, a fundamental norm of sovereignty that has been especially important in the non-Western world, the emerging powers display both similarities and differences. The BRICS countries, despite the differences in their political systems, appear to be somewhat united when it comes to state sovereignty. Brazil has strong pro-sovereignty attitudes similar to China and India. This addiction to Westphalian sovereignty raises questions about the contribution of the emerging powers to global governance, since some of the more pressing challenges to it, such as climate change and global financial volatility, require intervention in domestic affairs. As Hurrell notes, in dealing with "foreign policy and the governance challenges that states face [today] . . . climate change, stable trade rules, a credible system of global finance – necessarily involves not only cooperation but also rules that involve deep intervention in domestic affairs."[30] Among the emerging powers, China seems to be most interested in introducing new norms drawn from its own history and culture. For example, Yan Xuetong has proposed such principles as "benevolence" and "righteousness" that might complement the extant rules of "equality," "fairness," and "justice," and challenge hegemonic orders (mainly the US-led type) in international relations. For instance, "righteousness" (which he attributes to Mencius) stresses that "one's behavior must be upright, reasonable and necessary." This he sees as an essential corrective to the formal notion of democracy. "In international politics, democratic procedures may provide legitimacy for actions of a state but not necessarily guarantee the justness of such actions." Righteousness "requires justice in the contents of state actions." Here justice means benevolence toward the weak, where there is an imbalance of power. As an example, he asserts that "democracy only gives the right of independent development to weak nations whereas justice requires that developed countries provide assistance to developing ones."[31]

Despite their democratic credentials, India, South Africa, and Brazil have made common cause with China and Russia. South Africa, despite having gone through democratization with initial enthusiasm about its promotion, has become noticeably reticent in opposing authoritarian regimes in Africa, partly due to traditional ties between the ruling African National Congress and African leaders like Mugabe and the now deceased Gaddafi, and possibly also because of the ruling ANC party's investments in countries such as Angola and Zimbabwe. Indonesia has adopted a policy of democracy promotion, but it is a soft approach, supporting political change in Burma and establishing a dialogue over democratic ideas and practices through the Bali Democracy Forum.

There have been some recent developments indicating that the normative gap between the established and emerging powers over sovereignty and non-intervention may be narrowing. While China and Russia adopt a much more cautious attitude toward such interventions, South Africa and Nigeria have led the way in turning Africa's staunching non-interventionist stance to one that has allowed a number of collective interventions, including humanitarian interventions. While their dilution of non-intervention should not be overstated, the developing countries, including the emerging powers, are showing signs of being more interested and involved in rule-making, as well as contributing to some of the newer and more progressive norms of world order. The evolution of the R2P is a case in point. It is not well known that many African diplomats and political leaders were not only sympathetic to the R2P idea, but played a role in its development.

The origin of this idea of "responsible sovereignty" is usually credited to Francis Deng,[32] a Sudanese diplomat who once worked at the Washington DC-based think tank the Brookings Institution. In a collaborative project, Deng and his colleagues proposed that "those governments that do not fulfill their responsibilities to their people forfeit their sovereignty. In effect, the authors redefine sovereignty as the responsibility to protect the people in a given territory."[33]

Well before the R2P acquired a global prominence with the release of the report of the International Commission on Intervention and State Sovereignty (ICISS) in December 2001, key African leaders in South Africa and Nigeria had advocated collective intervention in response to African humanitarian problems. Nigerian President Olusegun Obasanjo argued as early as in 1991 that "An urgent aspect of security need is a re-definition of the concept of security and sovereignty . . . we must ask why does sovereignty seem to confer absolute immunity on any government who (sic) commits genocide and monumental crimes." And in 1998, South African President Mandela told his fellow leaders: "Africa has a right and a duty to intervene to root out tyranny . . . we must all accept that we cannot abuse the concept of national sovereignty to deny the rest of the continent the right and duty to intervene when behind those sovereign boundaries, people are being slaughtered to protect tyranny."[34]

The ICISS was co-chaired by Mohamed Sahnoun, an Algerian diplomat. Sahnoun himself called the R2P "an African contribution to human rights."[35] The African Union Constitutive Act is the first example of an international organization that has enshrined the R2P into its founding document. It recognizes the "right of the Union to intervene in a Member State pursuant to a decision of the Assembly in respect of grave circumstances, namely war crimes, genocide and crimes against humanity."[36] While other regions of the world, notably Asia, have been less receptive to R2P, misgivings about the norms mainly concern its manner of application, including its potential for abuse in the hands of Western powers, rather than the norm itself.

Prospects

A fair assessment of the role of emerging powers suggests that they do face a number of limitations in reshaping global order. The acknowledged members of this club lack sufficient cohesion to make the most of the opportunity presented by the global power shift. At the same time, they carry the risk of creating a new global elitism through clubs such as the BRICS and the G-20, at the expense of those who have provided other types of leadership. Their role in creating new principles of global governance is marred by a continuing emphasis on traditional norms of state sovereignty. Despite their limitations, the emerging powers do challenge the existing inequities in an international order hitherto dominated by the West. They also introduce a healthy diversity of cultural and intellectual traditions to an international system that has previously been derived mostly from the Western political and intellectual traditions (such as the Greco-Roman and the Enlightenment). It is unlikely that they would passively acquiesce with Western dominance of global rule-making and order-building in the twenty-first century, or that they would be co-opted into the existing liberal hegemonic order led by the US, without substantial concessions. At the same time, the emerging powers are not an adequate force by themselves to create a credible alternative. One reason for this is the regional context of their rise, which can either enhance or constrain their global leadership ambitions and potential. That context, alongside the role of regional coalitions and institutions in shaping global order, is a necessary part of the complex equation in thinking about our future as the American World Order ends.

– 5 –

Regional Worlds

The idea of a regionalized world order is not new, but deserves renewed attention in the context of the debates over the future of world order. Some proponents of the American-led liberal hegemony either ignore or fear regionalism and regional order building unless it is the EU or NATO. They associate regionalism with "regional blocs" – a shorthand for the breakdown of the liberal international order, rather than a building bloc of world order, The growing number and variety of regional political/ security and economic arrangements undercut their belief in the universality of liberal ideas and architecture, a belief that lay behind President Roosevelt's rejection of British Prime Minister Winston Churchill's advocacy of a regionalized post-World War II global security architecture.[1] Churchill had proposed the creation of three regional councils covering Europe, the Americas, and the Pacific, respectively, for organizing the post-war architecture. In opposing his plan, Roosevelt worried that the councils could encourage global fragmentation and might develop into competing power blocs jostling with each other for supremacy, thereby replicating a global version of the nineteenth-century European balance of power system blamed for two world wars. His preference was for a single universal organization to provide collective security: all for one and one for all. Did he also feel that a single organization would be easier for the US to manage and control? Evidently, the US president did not have the benefit of witnessing the birth of the European Economic Community, a different form of regionalism than the nineteenth-century alliances that he feared.

The nature and purpose of regionalism and regional orders, whether in Europe or elsewhere, have changed and broadened considerably since World War II. Not only have regional groups proliferated, but they have also embraced new roles and displayed considerable variations in terms of their designs and functions.[2] The notion of "regional worlds," coined by a now defunct project at the University of Chicago,[3] captures this broader, inclusive, open, and interactive dynamic of regionalism and regional orders, as opposed to the narrow and outmoded conception of regionalism of the nineteenth century that Roosevelt rejected and that contemporary proponents of liberal hegemony worry about.

From a regional world perspective, regions are not fixed geographic or cultural entities, but dynamic configurations of social and political identities. Moreover, regions are neither wholly self-contained entities nor purely extensions of global dynamics. "Multiple regions overlap and contradict one another to form complex webs of power, interaction and imagination that are constantly in motion."[4] The regional world perspective is not just about the internal dynamics of regions. Regions not only self-organize their economic, political, and cultural interactions and identities, but also contribute to global order. As Arjun Appadurai puts it, regions "are not just places, but are also locations for the production of other world-pictures, which also need to be part of our sense of these other worlds."[5] In other words, the regional-worlds perspective is an inside-out as opposed to an outside-in view of world politics.

The idea of regional worlds parallels the literature on "new regionalism."[6] A key difference between "old" and "new" regionalism is the comprehensiveness and multidimensional nature of new regionalism as opposed to the narrow and specific focus (strategic and economic) of the old. Another difference is that the former assumes the dominant role of hegemonic actors (or "hegemonic regionalism" created from "outside" and "above"), while the latter stresses the "autonomous" nature of new regionalism (from "within" and "below").[7] The creation and maintenance of regional institutions are not dominated by a single power. Instead, the sources and agency of ideas and approaches regarding order are diffuse and shared among actors. This concept not only differs from the hegemonic stability theory, as discussed in chapter 3, but also from the notion that multilateralism is a unique product of post-war *American* hegemony. Some regional orders may reflect hegemonic power and purpose, but my idea of regional worlds challenges the top-down view of power-constructed regions commonplace in the international relations literature. Regional worlds may emerge without hegemonic organization or even in resistance to it. In any case, any hegemonic construction of regional worlds is challenged by countervailing material and ideational forces. In regional worlds, "Power matters, but local responses to power may matter even more in the construction of regional orders."[8]

The liberal hegemonic approach to world order reflects a deep normative desire for universality. Yet this idea of universality ignores the varieties of actors, approaches, and experiences – including approaches to sovereignty and security – at the regional levels around the world.[9] The regional world perspective challenges this bias. Nonetheless, by using the term "regional worlds," I do not claim that the world is being divided into regions or that regions and regionalism are becoming the sole driving forces and operating sites of global order. While regions and regionalism are important trends in world politics, "regional worlds" is basically a metaphor to capture the multiple, diverse but cross-cutting foundations and drivers of global order. Instead of a singular, traditional notion of universality, the idea of regional worlds speaks to a pluralist conception of global order.

Regions under Liberal Hegemony

A good deal of our understanding of regions and regionalism was written against the backdrop of America's post-cold war ascendancy. Now with the unipolar moment over and the future of American hegemony under question, a fresh look at the changing forms of regionalism and regional order is warranted.

Historically, regions and regional orders have been influenced by powerful actors. Great powers have defined the boundaries of regions and even named them. The British did this during their heyday as the global hegemon. Consider the term "Southeast Asia." This term was almost unheard of before Lord Louis Mountbatten of Britain, the regional hegemon east of Suez, was appointed to head a newly formed military command established by the Allied Powers to fight the Japanese in Asia during World War II. Some of the most common terms for regions – "Near East," "Far East," "Middle East" – are also legacies of British imperialism. The US has also had its share of defining and naming regions for geopolitical reasons, such as "Southwest Asia" or the more incongruous notion of "Afpak."

While some American leaders distrusted the idea of sharing the authority of the UN with regional arrangements for peace, the US was pushed by the cold war to create regional arrangements under its own security umbrella. These might be classed as hegemonic regionalism, and included cold war alliances such as NATO, SEATO, and the Central Treaty Organization (CENTO). Only NATO survives today. Hegemonic regionalism in the developing world proved to be especially fragile. US hegemony also shaped economic regionalization sometimes through allied states like Germany and Japan, as documented in Katzenstein's book *A World of Regions*.[10] Regional order in Europe and East Asia is attributed to the provision of collective goods provided by American hegemony, such as protection against the communist threat during the cold war, together with US aid and access to the American market.

But, as mentioned in chapter 3, the US has been selective in its support for regionalism around the world. For reasons of power, interest, and prejudice,[11] it supported multilateralism in Europe directly through NATO (and indirectly through the European Community), while pursuing bilateralism in Asia. On occasion, it even went a step further, actively opposing nationalist inspired regionalism and inter-regionalism in Asia and Africa, which had developed independently from the strategic purpose of US hegemony and refused to submit to it. Thus, as discussed in chapter 4, the Eisenhower administration, with the active connivance and support of Britain, tried to manipulate the 1955 Asia–Africa conference in Bandung by first encouraging its allies to frustrate the goals of the leading Asian regionalists of the day, Nehru and Sukarno.[12] The US had no direct hand in the creation of regional bodies in the Middle East and Africa, such as the League of Arab States or the Organization of African Unity (OAU, which in 2000 became the African Union – AU). To a large extent, these groups were rather anti-American during their formative years, especially the Arab League during Nasser's rule in Egypt. The US enjoys greater influence within the Organization of American States (OAS), but here too the grouping was viewed by many of its members as a means to counter American hegemony.

What are the consequences of the end of unipolarity for regionalism and regional orders? Many of the currently fashionable terms to describe the future world order, as already discussed in chapter 1, for example, "non-polar," "post-American," "neo-polar," etc., underplay the regional context of world politics and security. Will we see a perceptible decline in the ability of the US to shape regional orders, institutions, and production structures around the world? Would there be a growth of regional institutions and orders that are not beholden to American power and purpose? In East Asia, regional production networks are increasingly centered around China rather than Japan, the pre-eminent American ally in Asia. In Europe, the growing demand for an autonomous or semi-autonomous defense identity may be another, albeit limited, example of such a challenge to US hegemony. It is useful here to keep in mind the faultline that emerged between Germany under Gerhard Shroeder and France under Jacques Chirac, on the one hand, and the Bush Jr White House, on the other, over the invasion of Iraq in 2003. In East Asia, the US ability to shape regional institutions, never all that strong, was undermined by the advent of East Asian regionalism, some versions of which (such as former Malaysian Prime Minister Mahathir Mohammed's idea of an East Asian Economic Grouping – EAEG – later renamed East Asian Economic Caucus – EAEC), excluded the US, even though the US has now joined the East Asian Summit.[13]

Regionalism's Changing Purpose and Relevance

Some of the more thoughtful analyses of the changing world order recognize the importance of regionalism, but examples of this are not perceived as hegemonic constructs. The *EUISS 2030 Report* (discussed in chapter 2) sees regionalism as a "vector of power." "The capacity to build regional cooperation groups to promote peace and social development will be crucial in determining the regional influence of states."[14] Regionalism is especially important to the international role of the "middle powers" such as Egypt, Nigeria, South Africa, and Indonesia, in enhancing their influence. In Asia, regionalism is a crucial factor in shaping peaceful relations between ASEAN and China, as well as between the US and China in Southeast Asia. While China and India are deemed by the report to be too large to engage in regional integration schemes with smaller states for economic benefit, regionalism is an important factor in their legitimacy as aspiring great powers. Regionalism through MERCOSUR and wider South American cooperation may be the key to Brazil's quest for great power status, without affording it any opportunity for regional hegemony.

The American *NIC 2030 Report* speaks of "[e]conomic trends, especially the likely growth of intraregional trade, [that] point to greater regional integration, suggesting the possibility of a world order built more around regional structures."[15] One rather unusual aspect of the "New American Moment" speech by the US Secretary of State Hillary Clinton, in September 2010, was the amount of space devoted in it to regions and regional organizations. Declaring that "Few, if any, of today's challenges can be understood or solved without working through a regional context," Clinton mentioned "region" (including "regional," "regionally," "regions," etc.) no less than 24 times in that speech. There is an entire section on "Strengthening Regional Architecture" (excluding discussion of NATO, which is under a separate preceding section on alliances, although NATO is basically a regional organization), which is longer than that on "Global Institutions in the 21st Century." Also, in discussing the role of emerging powers, Clinton warned that "Countries like China and Brazil have their own notions about what regional institutions should look like, and they are busy pursuing those ideas." This is another reason why the US needs to "remain robustly engaged and to help chart the way forward" in shaping regional architecture.[16]

The importance of regionalism and regional orders is further underscored by the fact that many of the emerging powers of today have been and are likely to remain fundamentally embedded in their regional strategic and economic contexts. Russia, for example, has been reduced to a regional hegemon, with its true influence confined to the Caucasus, the Baltics, and central Asia (although here it is facing serious competition from China). Brazil, South Africa, and Nigeria are also essentially regional players. None of these countries, or India and Japan, are likely to become true global powers in the sense the US and the USSR were during the cold war, or that European powers such as Spain, Britain, and France were (to varying degrees) when they controlled vast colonial empires. The EU is also essentially a regional actor: its influence beyond Europe is marginal.

In such a world, regions are likely to test the limits of power projection by the old or the rising powers. These powers will have a limited ability to influence distant regions because of the countervailing local influence of other regional powers. The US may be an exception but, even here, it is hard to see the US decisively shaping the strategic and economic future of Asia without cooperation from China, Japan, or India, or over the strong objection of any of them.

As already noted, the relevance, nature, and purpose of regionalism are changing in significant ways. The end of the cold war led to a redefinition of regions. In the 1960s, 1970s, and 1980s, the emergence of a number of subregional groups such as the GCC and ECOWAS indicated that regional boundaries, coinciding with macro-regional groups such as the Arab League, OAS, and OAU respectively, were too wide to address the specific security concerns of states. The end of the cold war, in contrast, led to a demand for the widening of regional boundaries established by subregional frameworks. In Southeast Asia, the anti-communist-oriented ASEAN was deemed too narrow a framework for the task of regional reconciliation necessary for regional security in view of the prospective settlement of the Cambodia conflict; thus it moved quickly to bring into its fold the communist Indochinese countries. In the economic sphere, Southeast Asia or East Asia was deemed too narrow a framework to manage the actual structure of regional economic interdependence. Hence the idea of Asia-Pacific was pushed to the fore to organize the Asia-Pacific Economic Cooperation (APEC). These changing regional boundaries brought new relevance to regional cooperation that could not be appreciated by looking only at the early post-war models of regional cooperation.

Second, regional organizations all over the world have taken on new responsibilities and functions. In the early post-war period, the main roles of the larger macro-regional organizations such as OAS, Arab League, and OAU consisted of pacific settlement of disputes, while those of the first wave of subregional groups such as the European Economic Community, Central American Common Market, and the East African Community focused on economic integration.[17] While the West European model of regionalism tried to separate economic and security issues for a long time (because of the existence of NATO with whom many EU members retain overlapping affiliations), regional organizations in the developing world learnt early that economic cooperation could not be meaningfully separated from political and security cooperation.[18] Hence ASEAN, ECOWAS, GCC, and SADC have become essentially multipurpose institutions, combining both economic and security roles and extending the latter to peacekeeping, peace-building, and humanitarian assistance and intervention. APEC was originally created to liberalize trade and manage economic interdependence in the Pacific, but it quietly developed a role in security, both as a venue for consultations on neighborhood conflicts (such as East Timor) and as a framework for addressing the transnational dangers such as terrorism. The New Partnership for African Development (NEPAD) has combined development and security goals in the form of three core initiatives: peace and stability, democracy and political governance, and economic and corporate governance.

Third, areas where regionalism has had a limited presence have seen the proliferation of entirely new institutions. Asia was the only continent not to have developed a macro-regional grouping in the immediate aftermath of the end of the cold war and decolonization. The founding of the ASEAN Regional Forum (ARF) in 1994 filled this gap. The ARF is to some extent a unique regional organization. It is the only regional group to bring together all the great powers of the contemporary international system. Yet at the same time it is led by ASEAN, a group of weaker Asian countries. South Asia and Central Asia, which lacked any form of regionalism, saw the establishment of subregional groupings in 1985 (South Asian Association for Regional Cooperation – SAARC) and 2001 (the Shanghai Cooperation Organization – SCO), respectively.

Fourth, regional organizations are reorienting and retooling themselves in order to respond to new transnational challenges. NATO had a clear collective defense function from its very inception, but it moved rapidly to broaden its role, and thereby retain its relevance, in the post-cold war period by embracing humanitarian intervention (Kosovo) and later counter-terrorism (Afghanistan). ASEAN's development of an ASEAN Political-Security Community in the past decade was largely in response to transnational dangers: terrorism, piracy, and pandemics such as the Severe Acute Respiratory Syndrome (SARS). The ARF has undertaken a number of initiatives for suppressing terrorist finance, promoting maritime security cooperation, and enhancing capabilities for humanitarian assistance in natural disasters in East Asia. Dealing with terrorism, financial volatility, climate change, energy supply, movement of people, and other transnational challenges has become routine for regional institutions all over the world.

Fifth, while issues of sovereignty and non-intervention remain a barrier to regional security cooperation, important changes are evident here as well.[19] NEPAD, a framework strongly backed by South Africa, has sought to move beyond Westphalian sovereignty by adopting a "peer review mechanism." Also, African regional and subregional groups such as ECOWAS, SADC, and AU have undertaken a number of collective interventions that would have been unthinkable in the past, when sovereignty and non-intervention were deemed sacrosanct. One important aspect of the willingness of regional organizations to go beyond the traditional view of state sovereignty is to be found in the Inter-American Democratic Charter adopted by the OAS in 2001. The charter makes a normative commitment to the promotion of democracy, as opposed to the traditional defense of state sovereignty. It permits collective action in defense of democracy not only in the case of coups, but also in situations of anti-democratic and unconstitutional "backsliding" by elected rulers. Even in Southeast Asia, despite the persistence of the non-intervention mindset, ASEAN has set up Asia's first regional inter-governmental human rights mechanism.

Finally, the traditional distinction between regionalism and universalism is becoming obsolete due to the growing practice of inter-regionalism.[20] The 1955 Asian-Africa Conference in Bandung, Indonesia, was a significant early example of inter-regionalism. Its 50th anniversary was held with another gathering of Asian and African leaders in Bandung. Regions meet routinely with each other and with outside powers. Examples include the Asia-Europe Meeting (ASEM) and the Forum for East Asia-Latin America Cooperation (FEALAC). The AU holds regular interactions with the EU, China, and India. A striking example of inter-regionalism can be found in Asia, where regional institutions are engaging not only the small and large players of Asia, but also of the whole world. The membership of the ARF and the EAS, developed around and led by ASEAN, includes all the major powers of the contemporary international system: the US, China, Russia, India, Japan, and the EU (in the ARF only). Also included are two of the key middle powers of the world, Australia and Canada (only in the ARF). These forms of inter-regionalism do not point to a fragmented world of regional blocs that the proponents of American hegemony are afraid of but, consistent with the regional world perspective, as a force against such fragmentation, and indeed as a stepping stone to a post-hegemonic stability. The rise of regionalism could be at least partly attributed to the limitations and weaknesses of global institutions, "a consequence of a system of global governance that increasingly seems to have fallen short of expectations."[21]

To be sure, regionalism is no panacea. Regional organizations, especially in the developing world, are constrained by lack of resources and institutional capacity. In Africa, regional collective action is constrained not so much by a lack of political will as by inadequate resources and capacity. In Asia, with such economically stronger states as Japan and China, the lack of political will resulting from inter-state mistrust and the non-intervention norm remains a more important barrier to regional peacekeeping and humanitarian intervention. Another obstacle to regional governance has to do with the fear and distrust of local hegemons, that is, India in South Asia, Nigeria in West Africa, South Africa in southern Africa, and China in East Asia (more on this in the last section of this chapter).

Some Western leaders and analysts oppose regionalism, especially regional trade arrangements, by casting it as a force for global fragmentation. In the early 1990s, the establishment of the European Single Market and signing of the North American Free Trade Agreement (NAFTA), as well as the Malaysian proposal for the EAEG, led to fears that a tripolar division of the world economy might supplant the global multilateral system. Yet such fears proved exaggerated. The growth of intra-regional trade did not occur at the expense of inter-regional trade; instead, the two grew together. For example, while the volume of trade among the USA, Canada, and Mexico increased after the advent of NAFTA, so did trade between NAFTA countries and East Asia. Similarly, rising intra-EU trade was accompanied by growth in the EU's trade with non-EU European Free Trade Area countries.[22]

Since then, bilateral and regional free-trade agreements have mushroomed around the globe. The number of regional trade agreements (RTAs) notified to the WTO jumped from 330 in July 2005 (out of which 180 were in force) to 546 (354 in force) by January 2013.[23] Part of the reason has to do with the stalemate in the Doha Round of WTO talks, and fears of being left behind if others entered into such agreements. But RTAs are also inspired by a sense among the political leaders that with shorter product cycles and longer lead times for multilateral agreements, regional agreements may offer a quicker pathway to free trade and investment.

The risks of regional trade arrangements include protectionism and trade diversion; as intra-regional trade increases, the volume of trade between that region and outsiders declines. Yet these risks can be overstated. Today, most regional groups are committed to "open regionalism," a concept that was developed in East Asia[24] but that also applies to other parts of the world. Open regionalism is understood mainly as non-exclusionary regionalism.[25] The idea implies that the outcome of trade and investment liberalization in the region will be the actual reduction of barriers, not only among regional economies *but also between regional and non-regional economies*. The very notion of open regionalism thus militates against any prospective breakdown of the liberal international trading order and the emergence of exclusionary regional trading blocs in Europe and North America.

The risk of global economic fragmentation posed by regionalism is reduced by the fact that successful regional trade groups tend to attract countries, including major economic players, from outside the region into participating in them, thereby promoting inter-regionalism and inclusivity. Also, large multinational companies, attracted by the lure of a larger trade and investment area that a regional agreement provides, tend to push for that grouping to operate within multilateral free-trade rules which provide them with the best guarantee of success. They not only push the member governments to resist protectionism, but also counter the pressure from local industries that oppose liberalization.[26]

Far from being a threat to the multilateral trading system, RTAs have complemented the WTO's role. Indeed, the WTO itself admits that regional trade arrangements benefit the multilateral trading system by enabling countries to negotiate rules and agree to commitments that go beyond existing multilateral agreements that can precede or pave the way for it, as in the case of services, intellectual property, environmental standards, and investment and competition policies.[27] For some governments, regional trade arrangements may be a catalyst for domestic economic reform, used by governments to signal commitment to openness, as was evident in the case of the former Soviet Bloc countries.[28] Regionalism has made it easier for countries to negotiate rules liberalizing the movement of capital, services, technology, and people.[29] Furthermore, promoting regional trade and investment relations can contribute to peace and security, as demonstrated by the members of ASEAN, something that their neighbors in South Asia are now emulating.

To sum up, the nature and purpose of regionalism and regional orders have changed fundamentally since World War II. Not only has the number of regional institutions grown, covering areas that had little previous experience in regionalism, but they have also adopted an ever widening variety of roles, including development, trade, finance, security, ecology, human rights, humanitarian relief, refugees, and pandemics. Some such roles have been undertaken relatively independently of the UN system, though most are in cooperation with it. But, in general, regionalism has remained "open" and has supported the global multilateral regimes, not threatened them. It thus makes little sense to dismiss regionalism and regional orders as a matter of competitive "bloc" formation – including the much feared but exaggerated challenge posed by "trade blocs" – signifying a fragmentation of world order.

Europe as the Model: Limits of a Hegemonic Idea?

Another key issue in considering the role of regions and regional institutions in world politics concerns the role of the EU as a model for regionalism and inter-regionalism for the rest of the world. Just as the literature on multilateralism has been heavily American-centric, much of the literature on regionalism was heavily Eurocentric, marked by a "widespread assumption . . . that in order to be 'proper' regionalism, a degree of EU-style institutionalism should be in place."[30] This inevitably leads to unfavorable comparisons between the EU's success and the failures and limitations of other regionalisms.

But the EU brand of integrative regionalism is under challenge as a paradigm for others to follow. In Asia, the trend toward regionalism resulted not so much through formal bureaucracy-driven trade liberalization, but from a "market-driven" process of transnational production. Transnational production networks and "natural economic territories" in Asia, in which factors of production – land, capital, technology, and labor – for a single product could be derived from, and located within, several national territories, constituted some of the clearest examples of such regionalization without formal inter-governmental regionalism, à la the EU.[31] In the case of Africa, regional linkages have been forged not through some grand schemes for an African Economic Community, but from transnational and subregional linkages along both formal and informal sectors of the economy.

The sources and trajectory of the EU have been so distinct from the rest of the world that the very idea of the

EU as a model makes little sense. Consider the differences between European and Asian regionalism, perhaps the two most important regions of world politics in the early twenty-first century. Asia's regionalism is much more consistent with the new regionalism and regional world perspective, and is marked by a near absence of supranational institutions like the European Commission or the European Court of Justice. It is much more informal and less legalized, based around the ASEAN way of consensus-based decision-making.

Broadly stated, the explanation for the differences between Europe and Asia rests on four main areas: history, foundational objectives, domestic political structures, and pattern of security relationship with external powers.

History

Europe is bound by a common religious and cultural tradition, believed to have originated from the legacy of the Roman Empire, which has evolved through centuries of diplomatic interactions through the balance-of-power system of the seventeenth–nineteenth centuries, manifesting in collective problem-solving mechanisms such as the Concert of Europe created in 1814. Asia, by contrast, is home to a cacophony of religions, cultures, and polities, with little record of multilateral interactions like that of the European Concert. Of course, this view can be refuted by pointing to the Chinese tributary system, discussed in chapter 3, which lasted until the advent of Western powers during the Qing dynasty. This was as much a diplomatic and security framework as an economic one, with the Chinese providing protection to weaker neighbors to fend off predatory neighbors (e.g., Malacca against Siam in the fifteenth century) as well as granting them the privilege to trade with China. But even then, the extent of these interactions and linkages was severely disrupted by the entry of Western powers, creating a major discontinuity in the evolution of a regional pattern of international relations in Asia.

Foundational objectives

European regionalism emerged from the ashes of two world wars that brought the continent to the brink of total annihilation. European regionalists, such as Jean Monnet and Friedrich Schuman, were motivated by a normative desire to prevent another European conflagration by taming the nation-state and its craving for absolute sovereignty. The ideas of the nation-state and sovereignty were new to Asia, and their importance was underpinned by an equally strong normative desire by Asian nationalists to avoid another long period of foreign domination and intervention. Asian regionalism was geared to advancing decolonization and promoting the nation-state by preserving state sovereignty, rather than overcoming it. This explains why Asia remains so strongly attached to the doctrine of non-interference and resists moves to create strong supranational institutions for economic and political integration.[32]

Domestic political structures

Europe, especially Western Europe, is home to "strong states," which after centuries of evolution through warfare and unity have reached a point of economic and political consolidation that is seemingly irreversible. Western European states all have strong liberal-democratic political systems. Asian states are "weaker," or what Katzenstein terms as "non-Weberian," where "rule by law" rather than "rule of law" tends to prevail.[33] The EU model assumes that strong states with democratic domestic politics are a necessity for regional cooperation to be viable. Yet both democratic and autocratic states in Asia have embraced regional cooperation. In fact, at its origin, ASEAN was essentially a grouping of authoritarian regimes, which nonetheless made a fairly strong commitment to regional unity. Now, ASEAN's political diversity has grown, but regionalism has not weakened. The lesson here is that Asia's regionalism is more adaptable to diversity in regime types, more in keeping with the situation in much of the non-Western world than the EU model.

Pattern of security relationship with external powers

While security in both Europe and Asia has been dependent on the US military presence and alliance commitments, Europe's has been a multilateral alliance structure, while Asia's has been framed by the so-called "hub-and-spoke" of bilateral alliances between the US and Japan, South Korea, Thailand, and the Philippines (along with Australia and New Zealand through the ANZUS Pact). While the EU has been developing its own "foreign policy and defence identity," this is hardly an autonomous enterprise, but draws upon a complementary and overlapping relationship with NATO. In Asia, there is no comparable complementarity between an American-led security structure and regional institutions that are led by ASEAN and that include as a full member China – the target of the "hub-and-spoke" system. This makes the EU hardly a model for security cooperation for Asia.

To varying degrees the above differences between European and Asian regionalisms can apply to other regions, such as Africa, the Middle East, and even Latin America, though the latter has an existing multilateral security structure (the Inter-American Defense System) that centrally features the US. This is not to say that regional institutions outside Europe are all similar in terms of their institutional features. Whether between Asia and Europe, or among the non-European institutions, regionalism displays a range of different institutional features. Yet, if judged in terms of their foundational objectives, which was to secure sovereignty from colonial powers and preserve it from outside intervention, non-European regional bodies have not been a waste, but have made important contributions to regional order. In Africa, they have helped maintained the stability of post-colonial boundaries, while in Latin America, they have contributed to the promotion of democracy. In Asia, they have contributed to stability by creating a framework for the socialization of former cold war adversaries – Vietnam and the original ASEAN, China and the US, China and India, China and Japan – and indeed all the major powers of the international system.[34]

Aside from the EU, the Organization for Security and Cooperation in Europe (OSCE) has provided important ideas and mechanisms for regional groupings in Africa and Asia. For example, at the OAU (now African Union) summit in 1999, President Obasanjo of Nigeria introduced a proposal on peace and security issues, which led to a new African peace and security initiative: Conference on Security, Stability, Development and Co-operation in Africa (CSSDCA), which was based on the OSCE model. The ARF was also partly inspired by the OSCE. The OAS has adopted several measures found in the OSCE process, while proposals have been mooted for an OSCE-type framework for the Mediterranean and the Middle East. A common emphasis of these frameworks is on confidence – and security-building measures (CSBMs). But adopting OSCE-style formal and legalistic CSBMs in non-European theaters has proven difficult, and the OCSE approach has had to be adapted and localized. The OSCE has also lost a fair bit of its shine in recent years, making its model less attractive to other parts of the world and promoting each region to search for its own pathways to peace and recon-ciliation.[35] And, since 2008, the EU's perceived inefficacy in handling the Eurozone crisis has diminished its attrac-tiveness as a model for regionalism for other parts of the world.

The Russian attack on Georgia in 2008 underscores the limitations of judging the performance of regional bodies in Asia and elsewhere on the basis of the European models. At the beginning of the post-cold war era, Russia

seemed less of a security challenge to its European neighbors than China appeared to its East Asia neighbors. Yet
China today is arguably better integrated into the Asian
regional institutions than Russia into European ones. In
Europe, the expansion of NATO, which George Kennan
regarded as "the most fateful error of American policy in
the entire post-cold-war era,"[36] turned out to be something of a self-fulfilling prophecy, triggering Russian paranoia. The Georgian crisis also says something about the
EU and OSCE, which despite the elaborate paraphernalia
of confidence-building, early warning, and preventive
diplomacy mechanisms, failed to stop what may turn out
to be one of the most serious breaches of international
order since the US invasion of Iraq. By contrast, Asia's
regional institutions, by discouraging an American-led
containment of China, by making multilateralism palat-
able to Beijing and using the resulting Sino-US restraint to
soften the region's balance-of-power geopolitics, have
prevented, at least to this day, a similar breakdown of
stability in the region. In other words, despite being consistently disparaged by Western scholars for their failure
to emulate European and Atlantic institutions, Asia's
regional institutions have arguably done a better job of
dealing with a rising China than Europe's in dealing with
Russia. Asia, which had long eschewed a NATO-like
alliance by rejecting multilateral collective defense, avoided
the type of provocation to China that NATO expansion
represented for Russia. NATO expansion contradicted
OSCE's doctrine of common security, or security with,
rather than against, the adversary. Asian regionalism actually imbibed it and followed it in spirit, if not in its legalistic form (CSBMs, high representatives, etc.) by offering
a genuine prospect for engagement to China. The provocation of NATO expansion aside, the OSCE's military
and political intrusiveness might have aggravated Russian
regime insecurity to an extent that ARF or other ASEAN-
based regional institutions could not do to Chinese regime
insecurity.

Of late, there has been much discussion of the EU as a "normative power," and of its role in diffusing the norms and processes of regionalism around the world, including in Asia. But this image of the EU suffers from a major contradiction. The vast majority of EU members are also part of NATO, which is nobody's idea of a civilian power. Only seven of the EU's 28 member countries are not members of NATO. Speaking the language of normative power while sticking to an expanding NATO allows EU members to have the best of both the worlds – speaking moralpolitik on certain type of world order issues such as human security and peace-building, while practicing realpolitik on matters of critical national and regional security. The fact that the former EU foreign and defense policy chief Javier Solana was also a former Secretary-General of NATO only compounded this perception, at least in the minds of non-Europeans. Unless there is meaningful separation between the foreign policy and security strategies of the EU and NATO, talk of the EU as a moral superpower will be unconvincing to outsiders.

The EU and ASEAN display different sorts of political context and normative purpose. ASEAN – essentially a group of relatively weak and developing states – is located in an area where its own security depends on the competition between the great powers. Therefore, ASEAN's normative role reflects its concern with preserving regional stability against great power dominance and intervention. By contrast, the EU, which includes several former great powers, and which can collectively count itself as a contemporary great power, seeks a normative role that aims to engage smaller players – many of which have serious domestic problems, inevitably highlighting the need for interference to change them. Whereas the EU employs its normative power primarily to influence and reshape the preferences and policies of states and regional bodies in the European periphery and in the non-Western world, ASEAN's normative role is concerned with engaging and socializing the great powers of Asia and the international system. This explains why it has been so difficult for ASEAN to move away from the non-intervention doctrine despite pressures such as the Asian financial crisis and growing transnational challenges. It also constitutes part of the reason why claims that the EU model of regionalism and the normative power of the EU have been major factors in shaping ASEAN's recent institutional development, including the ASEAN Charter and its human rights body, are not very convincing.

The differences between the EU and the regionalisms of the rest of the world should not be exaggerated. In some respects, Asian approaches to multilateral diplomacy might be closer to that of the EU than to that of the US. A few years ago at the height of the unipolar moment, Robert Kagan argued that Europeans disagree with America's "culture of death," that is, its tendency to view the world in "good versus evil" terms, its "warlike temperament," and its penchant for "coercion" and "unilateralism" over diplomacy and cooperation to attain national objectives. In this respect, both Europeans and Asians shared a common fear of these aspects of US hegemony at its highest post-cold war point. Both Asian and EU members (with the notable exception of Tony Blair's Britain) opposed the George W. Bush era American unilateralism. Kagan holds that, compared to Americans, Europeans are "more tolerant of failure, more patient when solutions don't come quickly." They eschew "finality" in international affairs, prefer "negotiation, diplomacy, and persuasion," and emphasize "process over result."[37] These observations have some resonance for Asian and other regional institutions as well. But what is clear is that the EU does not hold the monopoly over successful pathways to regionalism and regional order-building. Today, there is a growing recognition that effective regional cooperation need not follow a single model, derived from the European experience. The proliferation of regional groupings and the expansion of their scope and purposes have not been instances of simple diffusion of the European models and approaches to other parts of the world.

The Rerun of Hegemonic Regionalism?

One of the more important issues concerning the role of regional security arrangements in the emerging world order is whether they would remain under hegemonic control. In Europe, the principal multilateral security arrangement, NATO, has been the pre-eminent form of "hegemonic regionalism" in the sense that it existed, and continues to exist, within the purview of American hegemony. Regional security arrangements geared toward collective defense, and operating under the security umbrella of a great power, were never very popular in the developing world, as attested by the experience of the SEATO and CENTO. Even collective security and defense frameworks envisaged under the auspices of large multipurpose regional bodies such as the Arab League and OAS, or the OAU/AU, were hardly credible for the security of their members. In the third world, the term "regional security arrangements" invariably meant mechanisms for the peaceful settlement of disputes rather than collective defense.

The end of the cold war has diminished the appeal of a NATO-style of hegemonic regionalism. After the quick death of the Warsaw Pact, NATO has survived predictions of its early demise in the post-cold war era. But to ensure its continued relevance, it has had to embrace roles that had more in common with cooperative security organizations than collective defense in its classical sense. If NATO did not exist, it is doubtful that anyone would invent it today. Despite concerns over the growth of Chinese military power, the likelihood of there being an Asian NATO is slim for the foreseeable future.

This leads to another question about the future of regionalism: whether the end of unipolarity will open a space for the emergence of regional hegemonies, such as in East Asia under China, South Asia under India, the Caucasus and Baltics under Russia, southern Africa under South Africa, West Africa under Nigeria, and South America under Brazil. Mearsheimer argues that all aspiring great powers seek to achieve regional hegemony, a goal more necessary and attainable than global hegemony.[38] To Mearsheimer, China is the obvious candidate for such regional hegemony in the post-cold war period.[39] But Mearsheimer, who once warned that the post-cold war multipolar Europe would go "back to the future," was wrong about Europe, and may yet be so about China.

There is little sign of such regional hegemonies emerging today. Instead, one of the key challenges facing the emerging powers is the gap between their *global status aspirations* and *regional legitimacy*. All BRICS and many G-20 members are regional power centers. Some (e.g., India in South Asia, China in East Asia, Russia in the Caucasus) have problematic relations with their neighbors over territorial disputes, unequal economic relations, and suspicions of hegemonism. These regional problems can embroil them or pull them down sufficiently to undermine their quest for global status and influence.

Moreover, a country's quest for status as an "emerging power" can undermine its regional engagement. There is always the temptation to "leapfrog" their unglamorous neighborhood in order to pursue the global glitz and prestige that membership in BRICS and G-20 brings. Such concerns have been raised in the case of Indonesia (a G-20 member) in ASEAN, and Brazil (which belongs to both BRICS and G-20). The challenge for emerging powers is to ensure that their global power ambitions do not come at the expense of regional restraint and representation.

The roles of the emerging powers when it comes to engaging with their neighbors fall into three broad styles. The first one may be called hegemonic/domineering. Previous and more extreme examples of this style can be found in the US Monroe doctrine in the western hemisphere during the nineteenth and early twentieth centuries, and in Japan's Greater East Asia Co-Prosperity Sphere concept around World War II. Today, this style might apply to Russia in its "Near Abroad" (Eastern Europe, the Baltic states, Caucasus, and Central Asia). A less extreme version, a domineering type if not an outright hegemonic one, may apply to India's role in South Asia until recently, and China's in Southeast Asia in the past few years. Nigeria's role in the ECOWAS is also relevant as a possible example of the domineering approach. A second style may be termed "accommodationist." This describes the regional relationships of Brazil, South Africa, and Japan today. Their neighbors still fear dominance by the powers, often because of memories of the past. But the powers have gone some way in reassuring their neighbors by pursuing cooperation through regional groups.

A third regional style may be termed "communitarian." Two examples of this style are Germany's place in the EU and Indonesia's place in ASEAN. In both these relationships, the powers had committed aggression against their neighbors in the past. But now they exercise a high degree of restraint toward them. The neighbors reciprocate this restraint by acknowledging the leadership status of the powers. For example, Indonesia's role in ASEAN has been likened to that of being in a "golden cage." Jakarta's restraint toward its smaller neighbors such as Singapore and Malaysia has led the latter to express a degree of deference to Indonesia as the "first among equals" in ASEAN. There has been no war between Indonesia and its immediate neighbors since ASEAN was founded in 1967, just after Indonesia's war against Malaysia had ended.

The nineteenth-century US approach (Monroe doctrine) of seeking global leadership while riding roughshod over one's immediate neighbors will not work for emerging powers of the twenty-first century. Regional conflicts and complications could stifle their quest for global leadership. Moreover, unlike the cold war period, when the global level dominated the regional level, in today's world, the regional and the global levels of interaction are highly interdependent. Without support from their own regional groups, the emerging powers might be seriously constrained in playing a global leadership role.

Some emerging powers, aware that their global aspirations require a degree of regional legitimacy, are playing more constructive roles in their neighborhoods. In Africa, South African dominance does have its critics, and the Pretoria-backed initiative NEPAD is viewed in some quarters as an instrument of South African hegemony. But without South Africa, the transition of OAU to AU might not have been possible. Nigeria's role in the intervention by the Economic Community of West African States (ECOWAS) in Liberia attracted resentment from other West African states, but it was crucial to the limited success of that and other ECOWAS peace operations since. In South Asia, fear of Indian dominance has stymied the development of SAARC, yet it is hard to see any meaningful progress of SAARC without India's involvement and support. Also, India's relationships with its neighbors have become much more positive in recent years. In East Asia, while Chinese attempts to dominate them might spell the doom of regional organizations, these will be meaningless without Chinese involvement. So far, China's role in Asian regional bodies has been largely responsible and constructive.

Some argue that East Asia is a more hegemony-prone region than Europe, where modern international order had been founded on Westphalian decentralization and balance-of-power politics. Two scenarios of a regional hegemony in Asia have emerged. The first assumes that China, as a great power, is likely to pursue regional hegemony and seek to establish a sphere of influence over its immediate neighbors, which might conceivably include Southeast Asia and Central Asia. As noted, some Western analysts like Mearsheimer already see evidence of China seeking such hegemony, arguing that only a thin line separates China's charm offensive (now depleted) and a Chinese Monroe doctrine.

The other scenario of hegemonic Asia is a benign one. As noted in chapter 3, such scenarios of a peaceful and prosperous Asia under Chinese hegemony (or a hierarchical order with China as the leading state), have been put forward by both Western and Chinese scholars, and policymakers.

But evidence to support either view is scarce. Instead of developing a geopolitical framework in the style of a Monroe doctrine, which would exclude the US, China is conscious of the limits and dangers of such an approach.[40] It accepts US military presence in the region as a fact of life. The benign hegemony scenario is not credible either. Many Asian states, whether larger players like Japan and India or smaller ones such as Vietnam and South Korea, are not bandwagoning with China, but are keeping a wary vigilance.[41]

The proliferation of regional institutions, their expanding functions covering both traditional and transnational issues, and the growing incidence of inter-regionalism, may introduce a healthy diversity and leadership into the emerging world order instead of the singular dominance of American power or the EU's legalistic and centralized model of cooperation. As Weber and Jentlesen argue, "What makes these [non-Western regional] relationships distinctive is that they neither oppose nor accept Western rules – instead they seek to render Western rules less relevant by routing around them."[42] They do make the world less American-centric, but far from heralding a global fragmentation or the rise of regional hegemonies, these regional worlds could be an essential foundation for sustaining a multiplex world order in the twenty-first century.

− 6 −

Worlds in Collusion

In his well-known book *The Post-American World*, Fareed Zakaria notes that "Among scholars and practitioners of international relations, there is one predominant theory about how and why international peace endures. It holds that the most stable system is one with a single dominant power that maintains order."[1] But as a long-time scholar of international relations theory with a reasonable idea of policy debates, I cannot find much support for this assertion, either in the academic or the policy literature, at least to qualify it as a "predominant theory." His restatement of the hegemonic stability theory, as discussed in chapter 3, has been challenged and discredited for its ethnocentrism and its limited ability to explain stability and change in world politics. There is growing recognition that the creation of maintenance of international order is much more complex and depends on a wider variety of actors and mechanisms.

Since the end of the cold war, international relations scholars, policymakers and public affairs pundits have offered a veritable medley of speculations about the future of world politics. The initial prognosis of many was a multipolar world akin to the European international system of the nineteenth and early twentieth centuries. While most greeted the end of the cold war, others believed that multipolarity would make the future of world order similar to Europe's past, along with the danger of major power rivalry that characterized it. They even expressed nostalgia about cold war bipolar stability, ignoring the regional conflicts and human catastrophes that occurred in the developing world.

With the US-led invasion of Iraq in 1991, arguments over whether multipolarity would prove more unstable than bipolarity were quickly overtaken by a new debate over the "unipolar moment." On the one hand, its proponents saw unipolarity as stable and lasting; all the US needed to do was to actively police and counter any potential challengers. Yet the unipolarity is vanishing sooner than its proponents had forecast, the most optimistic of which expected it to last as long as the cold war had. At the same time, those who had argued that the unipolarity would not last were wrong about how it might end. It was ended not by the rise of other powers, although this was a factor, nor by conservative isolationism. Rather, unipolarity carried within itself the seeds of its own demise: represented by the arrogance and unilateralism of the George W. Bush administration in the US. Its end was hastened not by isolationism but by adventurism.

It is not surprising that a good deal of the speculations about world order proved wrong-headed. They often drew their examples from European history and geopolitics. But the world was moving to a situation which had no precedent in human history: the simultaneous rise of a number of states existing in different locations which nonetheless were able to interact on a regular and sustained basis. While individual great powers had existed in different parts of the world through history, they had been in relative isolation from each other. Globalization and the attendant transport and communication revolution, and the emergence of global institutions, now make it possible for them to interact and affect international relations as a whole. The result is a world that can hardly be described in terms of the traditional Eurocentric jargon of polarity. By the time analysts were catching up to this realization, partly the result of another overblown narrative about the "rise of the rest," one core belief about American power was making a last stand, the idea of a liberal hegemonic order.

This perspective argues that while America may be in decline, the liberal order or liberal hegemonic order it created will persist and might even co-opt its potential challengers, including China. This view, despite usefully highlighting the benign aspects of American hegemony, is flawed in important respects. It offers an exaggerated view of the scope of the liberal hegemonic order and glosses over its darker side, which had produced significant resistance to that order even before the 9/11 attacks on the US. There is scant recognition of the role of other states and transnational social movements in constructing international and regional cooperation.

In this book, I have offered a number of arguments why the future world order is unlikely to be an American-led liberal hegemonic order even if America recovers from its present economic downturn and legitimacy crisis. The degree of US dominance of the world will decline, even if the US itself does not. The resulting order would not be American, or hegemonic or liberal, in the narrow sense of reflecting US interests and values.

What might replace the American World Order then? Any attempt to answer this question is bound to be speculative. But the idea of a multiplex world suggests two possible approaches to order that might come after the passing of the unipolar moment. The first may be called a global concert model; the second, a regional world model.

The idea of a concert assumes that the great powers have a special responsibility in the management of international order. While relations among the great powers remain competitive to a certain degree, they develop a common interest in preserving international stability. To this end, they develop rules, interactions, and institutions not only to reduce competition among themselves, but also to manage other conflicts affecting the international system as a whole. A concert is thus different from the hegemony of a single power, but it is also essentially a collective hegemony of a group of big powers.

In a new global concert, the US would need to share power and authority with the emerging powers. This requires giving up some privileges in return for their trust and cooperation in order to make the system work. America's relationship with the emerging powers is a critical component of any possible concert system.

The concert model, while not unproblematic, is more plausible than some of the overhyped notions about the "rise of the rest." Such views hold that while American and Western dominance is ending, the emerging powers would take over leadership positions in global governance. But the emerging powers are in no such position. While they may possess increasing material power (economic and military), they too have their own legitimacy deficits and authority limitations. Their capacity to lead global governance is constrained by domestic instability, as well as a lack, in several cases, of regional legitimacy. Instead of displacing the traditional great powers, the emerging powers are better understood in terms of their regional context: their capacity for global role would be determined by events and linkages in their respective regions.

The emerging powers neither represent nor exhaust the possibility of an alternative, or post-hegemonic, governance. The US and the international community need to take a broad view of who is an "emerging power," rather than simply focus on the BRICS.

At the same time, the idea of a global concert among the established and emerging powers confronts three main challenges. First, the emerging powers themselves are not a cohesive group – they suffer from intra-mural conflicts (e.g., India–China), as well as disagreement over reform of global institutions (such as the expansion of the UN

Security Council). Second, concerts require a degree of ideological convergence that is absent among the emerging powers, as well as between them and the established ones. Third, a concert is essentially a great power club. The weaker states are marginalized, or at best play a secondary role. When people talk about concerts, they often have the nineteenth-century European Concert of Powers in mind. The system worked well initially but declined thereafter, suffering an eventual collapse with the Crimean War of 1854. Unlike in the nineteenth century, international politics today demands a far greater degree of transparency, accountability, and democratic constitution and management, which an old-fashioned concert model would be ill-positioned to provide. This problem is compounded by the fact that the emerging powers have a potentially divisive impact on the global South, while their clubs with the old powers such as the G-20 itself have legitimacy problems. They are seen as members of a global financial cartel.

The second model of world order, one that is more consistent with the multiplex metaphor, is the regional worlds approach. This kind of regionalism need not be an alternative to universalism, but a stepping stone to it.

During the cold war, the US was selective in its support for multilateralism at the regional level, encouraging it in Europe while preferring bilateralism in Asia. Regionalist movements that fought colonialism, or pursued non-alignment, were either ignored or opposed. Hence, might the end of the American world order open space for a more autonomous development of regions, regional orders, and regionalisms around the world? What would such an order look like and how would these diverse regionalisms relate to each other?

The founders of the American-led liberal order, such as President Roosevelt, distrusted regionalism by equating it with competitive geopolitical blocs. Some contemporary proponents of a liberal world order worry about much the same. Yet, as discussed in chapter 5, the nature and purpose of regionalism and regional orders have changed fundamentally since World War II. Regionalism today is broader, inclusive, open, and interactive. Hence, it may be an opportune time for the US to engage more closely and meaningfully with regional groups. It is a far cry from the narrow and outmoded conception of regionalism from the nineteenth century that liberals worry about.

New forms of regionalism have emerged around the world, some formal and institutionalized, like the EU, others more informal and non-legalistic, like ASEAN. Regional groups have taken up a variety of new roles beyond their traditional functions such as trade liberalization and conflict control. Today, they are engaged in transnational issues such as climate change, humanitarian assistance and intervention, and financial cooperation. A key transition in the emerging world order could be that regional orders become less geared toward serving America's power and purpose,[2] and are more reflective of the interests and identities of the local actors. This is not to say there would be an emergence of alternative regional hegemonies, such as a Chinese regional hegemony in Asia. This is unlikely to materialize. China has serious limitations in terms of military reach and as a public goods provider. It lacks both an attractive ideology and a sufficient geopolitical restraint toward neighbors, which constrains its regional legitimacy. While the non-hegemonic forms of regionalism that are most likely to emerge cannot resolve all the global issues, no major issue can be resolved without action and response at the regional level. A multitude of regional worlds could well provide an important foundation of world order.

Recognizing regional worlds does not mean neglecting global institutions like the UN. In fact, regionalism can strengthen the UN. The greater push for regionalism might make the task of UN reform more urgent and likely. For the US, a greater regional engagement might facilitate more burden-sharing beyond what is possible through formal alliances such as NATO or its bilateral pacts in Asia. For example, through closer regional engagement, the US can better address a variety of transnational dangers by working with regional approaches. Moreover, a regional order-building approach would also help the US in dealing with the emerging powers. Many emerging powers are primarily regional powers. As such, they pursue different ways of dealing with their neighbors. The US and other rising powers can encourage and assist those regional actors and emerging powers that play a positive role, like Indonesia and South Korea, in regional peace and stability. At the same time, through greater regional engagement, they can constrain those who display a coercive attitude toward neighbors. Indeed, such an approach is already evident in the US policy toward East Asia and some variations of it can be employed toward other regions.

However, a purely regional approach to global order carries its own limitations and risks. Regional groups vary widely in terms of their institutional structure, legalization, and capacity to solve collective action problems. One cannot rule out some of them degenerating into spheres of influence under the orbit of rising powers. To remain open and complementary to the UN system, regionalism needs to be accompanied by the reform of global institutions. If global institutions are severely weakened by their lack of reform and democratization, then it might encourage a form of regionalism that is an alternative to, rather than a building bloc of, universalism.

It goes without saying that not only the US but also the emerging powers and regional actors need to redefine and adjust their roles to sustain a post-hegemonic multiplex world. For the US, this means sharing power, not monopolizing it, partly by making multilateral institutions that it has long dominated more democratic. The so-called emerging powers should not demand recognition without contribution. They need to support world order-building with a greater role in peacekeeping and development assistance, and show greater restraint toward their regional neighbors. Regional organizations should be empowered with more resources and sharing of best practices while remaining within the framework of open regionalism and cooperative security. Groups such as the EU, ASEAN, AU, and OAS should take a leading role. The UN Security Council should cede more authority to regional groups, at least in an informal way.

For those worried about the risk of global elitism in a G-20-type concert model, or the potential of fragmentation in a regional world framework, perhaps a hybrid between the concert and regional world models can be envisaged. This is precisely what the idea of a multiplex world is about. A multiplex order would see the established and emerging powers developing a better understanding of the regional context of the emerging powers, and forging closer associations with regional institutions and actors. This can be done in a variety of ways. The established and rising powers should hold high-level meetings and dialogues among the various regional groups, provide capacity building assistance by channeling some of their bilateral aid to regional groups, and, where appropriate, even seek membership – at least observer status – in regional groups around the world, while being sensitive to regional concerns about outside interference. At the same time, a multiplex world order would not be similar to the classical European concert, but one that is more inclusive and responsive to the needs of weaker states, and thus enjoy greater legitimacy.[3] Unlike a concert, a multiplex order does not marginalize the weaker actors. Instead, the powerful actors respect the autonomy of the weaker ones and work with them to better manage order. A multiplex order is the political order of a culturally diverse world that rests on political and economic interconnectedness, as well as institutional arrangements, relying not on the power or purpose of a single actor or mechanism, but of a range of actors. This leads to another, more important, question. Would the end of the American World Order be a good thing for anyone?

"How does the world look in an age of U.S. decline?" is the headline of a commentary by Zbigniew Brzezinski. His answer is: "dangerously unstable."[4] Liberals raise the specter of "1930s-style world of mercantilism, regional blocs, and bilateral pacts."[5] Most commentators – both realists and liberals – believe that the US decline will usher in a dangerous world. One key signpost of this deeply ingrained belief about the necessity of American preponderance is that most analyses of America's position and role in the world, even by those who accept the possibility of American decline, usually end up with policy prescriptions that tell American policymakers how to reverse the nation's crisis, and maintain or strengthen its primacy relative to the rising powers. For all his musings about a "post-American World," Zakaria makes his points mainly based on the words of Franklin Roosevelt, Ronald Reagan, John McCain, Daniel Patrick Moynihan, Tip O'Neill, Colin Powell, Mitt Romney, Rudy Giuliani, Lou Dobbs, and Tom Tancredo (ever heard of him?).[6] His opening line, "This is a book not about the decline of America but rather the rise of everyone else," may be forgiven for its oxymoronic feel. But the above lines can be more accurately rephrased, judging from his overall tone and especially his "six guidelines" for American leaders at the end of his book, as: "This is a book not about the decline of America, but rather about how it can still be the top dog and defeat its growing competition."

Suggestions to restore America's prestige and influence in world affairs are more useful when they offer a balanced narrative of the US role in the world during the past "American century," highlighting its benefits and contributions but also acknowledging its excesses and limitations. Presenting a less rosy narrative of the record of American hegemony and acknowledging the contribution of other actors, including the Europeans, the non-Western nations, and transnational social movements, in the making of world order would not invite ridicule or disrespect from others. It might actually induce greater respect and legitimacy for the future of US power in world politics.

By acknowledging the limits of the scope of liberal order, and appreciating the role of nationalism, regionalism, and the cultural underpinnings of security policies and dynamics in different parts of the world, the US can also promote a more inclusive approach to multilateralism, beyond the current American-centric narrative. As Weber and Jentlesen argue:

> Most no longer believe that the alternative to a US world order is chaos. The rules and norms of that order are subject to much more extensive and intensive debate than ever before. There also is visible a relatively new phenomenon of routing around it, marking a world without the West with its own distinctive set of rules, institutions, and relationships. It cannot be taken as a given that the optimal model for a just society is the American one.[7]

Other powers, old and new, and different regional groups of the world, will have their conceptions of, and approaches to, local and international orders. The growing importance of regionalism – not just in Europe, but in other areas and representing a variety of models and approaches – is another signpost of the end of the American World Order. These different worlds will have powerful incentives to collude, not just collide.

Moreover, there are good reasons why the decline of the US and the hegemonic order it built may be good for America itself. Here I accept and keep in mind that the most credible projections discussed earlier in this book suggest that the US will still be a major force in the twenty-first-century world, but without its hitherto undivided military, economic, and diplomatic dominance. The most obvious benefit of this situation is that there will be less chance of a repeat of the George W. Bush era of hyper-unilateralism, along with its damage to America's international reputation and domestic economy vitality. The US will seek multilateralism not out of magnanimity or benevolence, which are neither peculiarly nor durably American, but out of the sheer necessity of burden-sharing. A more humble and multilateral American foreign policy in a world where America is made to work for its status as a globally respected power is also likely to attract wider support, and render US leadership more legitimate. America would be more willing to accept the rise of the rest and work with them and regional bodies to address global challenges. A decline might even shake America's domestic politics and make it more amenable to compromises and consensus.

As with the notion of US decline, the picture of a reconstituted American hegemony is imprecise and uncertain. But one thing is clear: the answer to the current uncertainty over world order lies not in pining for the revival of American hegemony. The world may never again see the kind of global dominance by any single power as it once experienced under Britain and the US. Global governance and order in this post-hegemonic era will depend on multiple actors and cross-cutting drivers.

No future world order can be expected to be free from competition, conflict, and violence. But this does not necessarily mean that when the American-led liberal hegemonic order fades, order and cooperation collapses. Not only does this view ignore the limited physical and normative extent of the American World Order during the cold war, but also the selective and self-serving deployment of its principles and institutions, the coercive elements (alongside the consensual ones) of US leadership, and the contributions of other actors to global and regional order-building. A practical danger of viewing world order in excessively American-centric terms is that one loses sight of the other actors, instruments, and modalities of global peace and prosperity. A broader understanding of what constitutes world order, who are its makers and wreckers, and what conditions sustain or damage it, is long overdue.

World order depends not just on how America perceives and relates to the rest, but also on how the rest perceives and deals with American power. The emerging powers or regional institutions often want to shape America's policy toward them in directions that are not destabilizing but are more conducive to regional and global peace. This factor is not based on the logic of the balance of power; nor is it based on a community of liberal values. It may be inspired by a desire to keep the peace with America and in the world. It may also be inspired by a belief that global peace and security is not America's responsibility alone, and that America could do with some advice and help from others. A case in point is that of ASEAN members, worried about both China's rise and the adverse repercussions of a US containment strategy, who have simultaneously engaged all the major powers of the region and the world so as to induce strategic restraint and responsible conduct. For the liberal hegemony theory, peace depends on how a hegemon organizes the world after its own interests and values, and on the terms it sets that allow others to join the club. Yet global order may also be shaped by how the other actors, including the emerging powers, socialize a hegemonic actor (especially one that is no longer capable of ruling by absolute fiat) into their norms and institutions that are aimed at promoting peace and stability. This sort of thinking and approach is especially likely at a time when the world may be no longer in awe of America.[8]

Our perspectives on the past and the emerging world order should view it in terms of four dimensions: height, length, depth, and time. When it comes to height, or power, for example, a good deal of the debate over the post-cold war era – such as the unipolar moment, unipolar illusion, and unipolar stability – has been based mainly on the shifts in the distribution of material power, including the end of bipolarity or the rise and fall of the unipolar moment. While power distribution matters, it can hardly capture the complexity of world politics today. The question of length is also important. The idea of a liberal hegemonic order has neglected the role of regions and regional constructions of order in world politics; but regions are becoming crucial sites of conflict and cooperation in world politics. The issue of depth brings to the fore not only the quality of American leadership, but also the leadership potential and legitimacy of the emerging powers. The lack of a sense of time has led to highly questionable parallels between Europe's past and the world's future, even when Europe's past bears little resemblance to the global and regional dynamics of the twenty-first century. The four-dimensional perspective provides a broader, more comprehensive, and long-term picture of world order than the dominant idea of a liberal hegemonic order.

Notes and References

Chapter 1   A Multiplex World

1 "A Worrying New World Order," *The Economist* (September 11, 2008); Fareed Zakaria, *The Post-American World* (W. W. Norton, 2008); Richard Haas, "The Age of Nonpolarity," *Foreign Affairs* (May–June 2008); Charles A. Kupchan, *No One's World: The West, the Rising Rest, and the Coming Global Turn* (Oxford University Press, 2012).

2 John Ikenberry, *Liberal Leviathan: The Origins, Crisis, and Transformation of the American World Order* (Princeton University Press, 2011).

3 Here I borrow from Ruggie's account of multilateralism. In tracing the emergence of multilateralism, Ruggie observed, "Looking more closely at the post-World War II situation . . . it was less the fact of American *hegemony* that accounts for the explosion of multilateral arrangements than of *American* hegemony" (emphasis in original); John G. Ruggie, "Multilateralism: The Anatomy of an Institution," in Ruggie, ed., *Multilateralism Matters: The Theory and Praxis of an Institutional Form* (Columbia University Press, 1993), p. 8.

4 John K. Fairbank, ed., *The Chinese World Order* (Harvard University Press, 1968).

5 Paul Evans, "Historians and Chinese World Order: Fairbank, Wang, and the Matter of 'Indeterminate Relevance,'"

in Zheng Yongnian, ed., *China and International Relations: The Chinese View and the Contribution of Wang Gungwu* (Routledge, 2010), p.46.

6 Amitav Acharya, "State Sovereignty after 9/11: Disorganized Hypocrisy?," *Political Studies*, 55/2 (summer 2007): 274–96.

7 For an interesting comparison between Chinese and American orders, see Yuen Foong Khong, "The American Tributary System," *Chinese Journal of International Politics*, 6 (2013): 1–47.

8 For a debate over the Chinese World Order, see David C. Kang, "Getting Asia Wrong: The Need for New Analytical Frameworks," *International Security*, 27/4 (spring 2003): 57–85; Amitav Acharya, "Will Asia's Past Be Its Future?," *International Security*, 28/3 (winter 2003/04): 149–64.

9 Joseph S. Nye, "The Future of American Power: Dominance and Decline in Perspective, *Foreign Affairs*, 89/6 (November/December 2010): 2–12.

10 Joseph S. Nye, "Is America an Empire?," *Project Syndicate* (January 26, 2004).

11 Back in the 1990s, the Japanese diplomat Yukio Satoh had used the term "multiplex approach" to describe the coexistence of America's bilateral alliances and the emerging regional multilateral groups in the Asia-Pacific region. But Satoh did not view this as a theater or cinema, confining the term to regional institutions and alliances.

12 See *The Miriam Webster Dictionary* available online at: <http://www.merriam-webster.com/dictionary/multiplex>.

Chapter 2   The Rise and Fall of the Unipolar Moment

1 Charles Krauthammer, "The Unipolar Moment," *Foreign Affairs*, 70/1 (1990/91): 23–33.

2 Charles Krauthammer, "A Believer in a Robust U.S. Role," *International Herald Tribune* (March 23–4, 1991), p.6.

3 John Mearsheimer, "Back to the Future: Instability in Europe After the Cold War," *International Security*, 15/1 (summer 1990): 5–55.

4 Aaron L. Friedberg, "Ripe for Rivalry: Prospects for Peace in a Multipolar Asia," *International Security*, 18/3 (winter,

1993–4): 5–33; Aaron L. Friedberg, "Will Europe's Past be Asia's Future?," *Survival*, 42/3 (2000): 147–60.

5 William Wohlforth, "The Stability of a Unipolar World," *International Security*, 24/1 (summer 1999): 8.

6 Christopher Layne, "The Unipolar Illusion: Why New Great Powers Will Rise," *International Security*, 17/4 (spring, 1993): 5–51.

7 Ibid.: 7.

8 Steven Weber and Bruce W. Jentleson, *The End of Arrogance: America in the Global Competition of Ideas* (Harvard University Press, 2010); Kindle edition (Kindle Locations: 377–8).

9 "China 'To Overtake America by 2016,'" *The Telegraph* (June 24, 2013). Other sources think it will be around 2030, see the discussion later in this chapter.

10 Charles Krauthammer, "The Unipolar Moment Revisited," *The National Interest*, 70 (winter 2002/03): 5–17.

11 Wohlforth, "The Stability of a Unipolar World," p. 8.

12 Both Wohlforth and Layne are self-professed admirers of Waltzian neo-realism, which holds that the structure of the international system, rather than human nature or domestic politics, shapes international outcomes. Kenneth N. Waltz, *Theory of International Politics* (Addison-Wesley, 1979), p. 168.

13 Kenneth N. Waltz, "The Stability of a Bipolar World," *Daedalus*, 93/3 (1964): 882.

14 Waltz, *Theory of International Politics*, p. 168.

15 Waltz, "The Stability of a Bipolar World," p. 907.

16 John Lewis Gaddis, "The Long Peace: Elements of Stability in the Post-War International System," *International Security*, 10/4 (spring 1986): 104.

17 Mohammed Ayoob, "Regional Security and the Third World," in Mohammed Ayoob, ed., *Regional Security in the Third World* (Croom Helm, 1986), p. 14.

18 The "unipolar illusion" perspective did not equate the cold war with the "Long Peace" in the international system as a whole, but only with the "West's Long Peace"; Layne, "The Unipolar Illusion," p. 41. While it does not see unipolarity as durable, it sees its end as ushering in heightened instability in the international system.

19 Waltz, *Theory of International Politics*, p. 171.

20 John Mearsheimer, "Why We Will Soon Miss the Cold War," in Mark Charlton and Elizabeth Ridell-Dixon, eds, *Crosscurrents: International Relations in the Post-Cold War Era* (Nelson Canada, 1993), p. 16.

21 Dale Copeland, "Realism and Neorealism in the Study of Regional Conflict," paper presented at the conference on "When Regions Transform," McGill University, April 9, 2010.

22 John J. Mearsheimer, "Why We Will Soon Miss the End of the Cold War," *The Atlantic Online* (August 1990); at: <http://www.theatlantic.com/past/politics/foreign/mearsh.htm> (accessed November 13, 2013).

23 Karl W. Deutsch and J. David Singer, "Multipolar Power Systems and International Stability," in James N. Rosenau, ed., *International Politics and Foreign Policy* (The Free Press, 1969), p. 320.

24 Richard N. Rosecrance, "Bipolarity, Multipolarity, and the Future," in James N. Rosenau, ed., *International Politics and Foreign Policy* (The Free Press, 1969), p. 328.

25 Karl Deutsch and David Singer, "Multipolar Power Systems and International Stability," *World Politics*, 16/4 (1964): 390–406; Charles Kupchan, "After Pax Americana: Benign Power, Regional Integration, and the Sources of a Stable Multipolarity," *International Security*, 23/2 (fall 1998): 40–79.

26 Deutsch and Singer, "Multipolar Power Systems and International Stability," p. 318.

27 Barry Buzan and Ole Waever, *Regions and Powers: The Structure of International Security* (Cambridge University Press, 2003).

28 For scenarios of multipolarity in Asia, see Friedberg, "Ripe for Rivalry," and Barry Buzan and Gerald Segal, "Rethinking East Asian Security," *Survival*, 36/2 (summer 1994): 8–10. For a bipolar scenario, see Robert L. Ross, "The Geography of the Peace: East Asia in the Twenty-First Century," *International Security*, 23/4 (1999): 81–118; Something akin to unipolarity (or benign Chinese primacy) has been suggested by Kang, "Getting Asia Wrong," pp. 57–85.

29 Paul Kennedy, *The Rise and Fall of the Great Powers: Economic Change and Military Conflict From 1500 to 2000* (Random House, 1987).

30 Ezra Klein, "American Decline a Mirage in a World That's Rising," May 16, 2012; see: <http://www.bloomberg.com /news/2012-05-16/american-decline-a-mirage-in-a-world -that-s-rising.html>.

31 Christopher Layne, "US Decline," in Michael Cox and Doug Stokes, eds, *U.S. Foreign Policy*, 2nd edn (Oxford University Press, 2012), p. 23.

32 Linda Blimes, "The Financial Legacy of Iraq and Afghanistan: How Wartime Spending Decisions Will Constrain Future National Security Budgets," Faculty Research Working Paper Series, John F. Kennedy School of Government, Harvard University; at: <http://www.nytimes.com/2013/03/20/opinion/the-silver-linings-of-iraq.html> (accessed June 5, 2013).

33 Cited in Mark Urban, "Is the United States an Empire in Decline," BBC News, September 20, 2012, at: <http://www.bbc.co.uk/news/world-us-canada-19667754> (accessed June 5, 2013).

34 Robert Kagan, *The World America Made* (New York: Knopf Doubleday, 2012).

35 Looking at Kagan's source, the US Department of Agriculture database, I found that his data is similar to data that uses constant 2005 dollars, which even then shows a decline from 28.3 percent in 1999 to 26.04 percent in 2009 and 25.3 percent in 2012, whereas Kagan shows a decline from 28 percent in 1999 to 26 percent in 2009. Kagan derives his data from: USDA Economic Research Service, *Real Historical Gross Domestic Product (GDP) Shares and Growth Rates of GDP Shares for Baseline Countries/Regions (in Percent), 1969–2010* (updated December 22, 2010). My data is from the same source, but covers the 1969–2012 period and is updated on November 3, 2012; see: <http://www.ers.usda.gov/data-products/international-macroeconomic -data-set.aspx#.Ua8h3ZzgaSk> (accessed June 5, 2013).

36 Robert A. Pape, "Empire Falls," *The National Interest*, (January–February 2009), p. 7; Robert Pape, "Realities and Obama's Diplomacy," *Chicago Tribune*, March 8, 2009, p. 29.

37 Gideon Rochman, "America's Decline, This Time It Is Real," at: <http://www.foreignpolicy.com/articles/2011/01/02/think _again_american_decline?page=full> (accessed June 5, 2013).

38 Walter Russell Mead, "The Myth of America's Decline," *Wall Street Journal* (April 9, 2012).
39 Clyde Prestowitz, "The American Decline Debate," April 12, 2012, blog, at: <http://prestowitz.foreignpolicy.com/posts /2012/04/12/the_american_decline_debate>.
40 Charles Kupchan, "Is American Primacy Really Diminishing?," *National Journal* (March 15, 2012).
41 Kagan, *The World America Made*.
42 Joseph S. Nye, "Declinist Pundits," *Foreign Policy* (November 2012).
43 Ruchir Sharma, *Breakout Nations: In Pursuit of the Next Economic Miracles* (W. W. Norton, 2012).
44 Nye, "Declinist Pundits."
45 Clyde Prestowitz, "The American Decline Debate," April 12, 2012, blog, at: <http://prestowitz.foreignpolicy.com/posts /2012/04/12/the_american_decline_debate> (accessed June 5, 2013).
46 Ian Bremmer, "Five Myths About America's Decline," *The Washington Post* (May 3, 2012).
47 Charles Wolf, Jr., "The Facts About American 'Decline,'" *Wall Street Journal* (April 13, 2011).
48 "China's rapid and comprehensive transformation of its armed forces holds implications beyond the Asia-Pacific region." This build-up will "challenge our freedom of action in the region." Statement of Admiral Robert F. Willard, US Navy, Commander US Pacific Command Before the Senate Armed Services Committee on US Pacific Command Posture, March 24, 2010, at: <http://www.armed-services.senate.gov /statemnt/2010/03%20March/Willard%2003-26-10.pdf> (accessed June 5, 2013).
49 Wolf, Jr., "The Facts About American 'Decline.'"
50 "Economy: Developing Countries Set to Account for Nearly 60% of World GDP by 2030, According to New Estimates," at: <http://www.oecd.org/dev/pgd/economydevelopingcoun triessettoaccountfornearly60ofworldgdpby2030according tonewestimates.htm> (accessed June 5, 2013).
51 The World Bank, "Developing Economies Increase Share of Global Output," July 8, 2010, at: <http://data.worldbank. org/news/dev-economies-increase-share-of-global-output>.
52 "Developing Economies to Eclipse West by 2060, OECD Forecasts," *The Guardian Datablog*, available at: <http://

www.guardian.co.uk/global-development/datablog/2012
/nov/09/developing-economies-overtake-west-2050-oecd
-forecasts> (accessed June 5, 2013).

53 *Global Trends 2030 – Citizens in an Interconnected and Polycentric World* (The European Union Institute for Security Studies, May 2012).

54 US National Intelligence Council, *Global Trends 2030: Alternative Worlds* (2012).

55 Harinder S. Kohli, Ashok Sharma, and Anil Sood, *Asia 2050: Realizing the Asian Century* (Sage, 2011), pp. 47, 293.

56 Krauthammer, "The Unipolar Moment," p. 27.

57 Layne, "The Unipolar Illusion," p. 51.

58 Ikenberry, *Liberal Leviathan*, p. 32.

Chapter 3   The Myths of Liberal Hegemony

1 Ikenberry, *Liberal Leviathan*, p. 224.

2 Ibid., p. 6.

3 Robert Cox, *Social Forces, States, and World Orders, Approaches to World Order* (Columbia University Press, 1996).

4 Indeed, Ikenberry explicitly draws upon the arguments of HST regarding the hegemon's interest in and "ability to bear disproportionately the costs of providing international public goods such as an open world economy and a stable security order." Ikenberry, *Liberal Leviathan*, p. 143.

5 Isabelle Grunberg, "Exploring the Myth of Hegemonic Stability," *International Organization*, 44/4 (autumn 1990): 431.

6 Ikenberry, *Liberal Leviathan*, p. 70.

7 Robert Gilpin (with Jean Gilpin), *The Political Economy of International Relations* (Princeton University Press, 1987); Stephen Krasner, "State Power and the Structure of International Trade," *World Politics*, 28/3 (1976): 317–43.

8 For a critique of the ethnocentric bias of the hegemonic stability theory, such as Gilpin's contention that free trade is imposed by a "superior society," see Grunberg, "Exploring the Myth of Hegemonic Stability," pp. 444–8. The reference is to Robert Gilpin, *War and Change in World Politics* (Cambridge University Press, 1981), p. 129.

9 Duncan Snidal, "The Limits of Hegemonic Stability Theory," *International Organization*, 39/4 (autumn 1985): 579–614.

10 See: <http://www.sociology.org.uk/ws1k5.htm>.

11 New World Encyclopedia, at: <http://www.newworldency clopedia.org/entry/Metanarrative>.

12 Grunberg, "Exploring the Myth of Hegemonic Stability," p. 432.

13 Ibid., p. 433; David Calleo, *Beyond American Political Hegemony*, pp. 218, 220; Calleo and Rowland, *America and the World Political Economy*, p. 17, both cited in Grunberg, p. 432.

14 Ikenberry, *Liberal Leviathan*, p. 7.

15 "The End of the Cold War and the Soviet Union," at: <http://www.fsmitha.com/h2/ch33.htm> (accessed October 3, 2013).

16 Derek Thompson, "The Economic History of the Last 2000 Years: Part III," *The Atlantic* (June 22, 2012).

17 Ikenberry, *Liberal Leviathan*, p. 15.

18 Ibid., p. xiii.

19 Ibid., p. 6.

20 Ibid., chapter 6.

21 Ibid., p. 251.

22 Available at: <http://www.state.gov/secretary/rm/2010/09/146917.htm> (accessed June 5, 2013).

23 Ikenberry, *Liberal Leviathan*, pp. 26–7, 142.

24 Weber and Jentleson, *The End of Arrogance*.

25 Amitav Acharya, "Lessons of Bandung, Then and Now," *Financial Times* (April 22, 2005).

26 Miles Kahler, "Who Is Liberal Now? Rising Powers and Global Norms," paper prepared for the conference, *Why Govern: The Strategic, Functional and Normative Logics of Global Governance*, American University, Washington, DC, October 3–5, 2013.

27 Andrew Hurrell, "Power Transitions, Global Justice and the Virtues of Pluralism," *Ethics and International Affairs*, 27/2 (summer 2013): 189–205.

28 Amitav Acharya, "How Ideas Spread: Whose Norms Matter? Norm Localization and Institutional Change in Asian Regionalism," *International Organization*, 58/2 (spring 2004): 239–75.

29 Jorge Dominguez, "International Cooperation in Latin America: The Design of Regional Institutions by Slow Accretion," in

Amitav Acharya and Alastair I. Johnston, eds, *Crafting Cooperation: Regional International Institutions in Comparative Perspective* (Cambridge University Press, 2008), pp. 83–128.

30 Kathryn Sikkink, "Human Rights as Constitutive Norms of Global Governance," paper prepared for the conference *Why Govern: The Strategic, Functional and Normative Logics of Global Governance*, American University, Washington, DC, October 3–5, 2013.

31 Eric Helleiner, *Forgotten Foundations of Bretton Woods: International Development and the Making of the Postwar Order* (Cornell University Press, 2014).

32 Amitav Acharya, "Norm Subsidiarity and Regional Orders: Sovereignty, Regionalism and Rule Making in the Third World," *International Studies Quarterly*, 55/1 (2011): 95–123.

33 Joseph E. Stiglitz, "Some Lessons from the East Asian Miracle," *The World Bank Research Observer*, 11/2 (August 1996): 151–77; Richard Stubbs, "Asia-Pacific Regionalization and the Global Economy: A Third Form of Capitalism?," *Asian Survey*, 35/9 (September 1995): 785–97.

34 Francis Fukuyama, at: <http://en.wikipedia.org/wiki/Francis_Fukuyama>; *The End of History and the Last Man* (Free Press, 1992).

35 Weber and Jentleson, *The End of Arrogance*.

36 John Oneal and Bruce Russett, *Triangulating Peace: Democracy, Interdependence, and International Organizations* (W. W. Norton, 2000).

37 Edward Mansfield and Jack Snyder, "Democratization and the Danger of War," *International Security*, 20/1 (summer, 1995): 5–38; Jack Snyder, *From Voting to Violence: Democratization and Nationalist Conflict* (W. W. Norton, 2000).

38 Scott Sagan and Kenneth N. Waltz, *The Spread of Nuclear Weapons: An Enduring Debate*, 3rd edn (W. W. Norton, 2012).

39 Keith Krause, ed., *Culture and Security: Multiculturalism, Arms Control and Security Building* (Frank Cass, 1998); Amitav Acharya, "Collective Identity and Conflict Management in Southeast Asia," in Emmanuel Adler and Michael Barnett, eds, *Security Communities* (Cambridge University Press, 1998), pp. 198–227.

40 Ikenberry, *Liberal Leviathan*, p. 345.
41 Alastair Iain Johnston, "Is China a Status Quo Power?," *International Security*, 27/4 (spring 2003): 5–56; Amitav Acharya, "Can Asia Lead? Power Ambitions and Global Governance in the Twenty-first Century," *International Affairs*, 87/4 (2011): 851–69.
42 Johnston, "Is China a Status Quo Power?"; Acharya, "Can Asia Lead?."
43 Ikenberry, *Liberal Leviathan*, p. 344.
44 Kang, "Getting Asia Wrong," p. 66.
45 David C. Kang, *China Rising: Peace, Power, and Order in East Asia* (Columbia University Press, 2008).
46 Such a revival is implausible. See Amitav Acharya, "Will Asia's Past Be Its Future?"
47 Yaqing Qin, "Why Is There No Chinese International Relations Theory?" *International Relations of the Asia-Pacific*, 7 (2007): 313–40. Zhao Tingyang, *Tianxia tixi: Shijie zhidu zhexue daolun* [The Tianxia System: A Philosophy for the World Institution] Nanjing: Jiangsu Jiaoyu Chubanshe, 2005 (Translated for the author by Shanshan Mei).
48 To quote its most prominent advocate, Zhao Tingyang, *Tianxia* has four key elements: (1) *Non-exclusion*: or the "'exclusion of nothing and nobody' or the 'inclusion of all peoples and all lands'"; (2) *World Institution*: "the Zhou Dynasty chose the world, and not the state, as the starting point for political thinking"; (3) *democracy at international level*: domestic democracy without international democracy might lead to imperialist hegemony. "[A]n institution is good if and only if it can be applied on all political levels, from the most basic to the highest, and from local to worldwide dimensions, thereby leading to a universal political system"; and (4) *harmony versus sameness*: Harmony is "usually defined as reciprocal dependence, reciprocal improvement or the perfect fitting for different things, as opposed to the *sameness* of things." Zhao Tingyang, *Tianxia tixi: Shijie zhidu zhexue daolun*.
49 Wen Jiabao, "Turning Your Eyes to China" speech given at Harvard University, December 10, 2003. At: <http://www.fmprc.gov.cn/ce/ceun/eng/xw/t56090.htm> (accessed October 3, 2013). Yu Keping, "We Must Work to Create a Harmonious World," *China Daily*, May 10, 2007. At: <http://

china.org.cn/english/international/210305.htm>   (accessed October 3, 2013). Yu was a senior advisor to the Chinese leadership.

50 Yan Xuetong, "New Values for New International Norms," *China International Studies*, 38 (January/February 2013): 17.

51 Marcus Tourinho, "For Liberalism without Hegemony: Brazil and the Rule of Non-Interventon," paper prepared for the workshop on "Brazil and the Liberal Order," American University, Washington, DC, September 5–6, 2013, p. 14.

52 Oliver Stuenkel, "The Critique of Liberal Internationalism in Comparative Perspective: Brazil and the BRICS Nations," paper prepared for the Workshop on "Brazil and the Liberal Order," American University, Washington DC, September 5–6, 2013, p. 1.

53 Ivo Daalder and James Lindsay, "Democracies of the World, Unite," *American Interest*, 2/3 (January/February 2007); G. John Ikenberry and Anne-Marie Slaughter, "Forging a World of Liberty Under Law: U.S. National Security in the 21st Century," The Princeton Project on National Security, September 27, 2006, at: <http://www.princeton.edu/~ppns /report/FinalReport.pdf>; Robert Kagan, "The Case for the League of Democracies," *Financial Times* (March 13, 2008).

54 Kupchan, *No One's World*, p. 141.

55 Ibid., p. 87.

56 "The ICC in the Security Council," *Global Policy Forum*, no date. At: <http://www.globalpolicy.org/security-council /security-council-as-an-institution/the-power-of-the-veto -0-40/the-veto-and-the-icc-in-the-security-council.html> (accessed October 3, 2013).

57 Hillary Clinton, "The New American Moment," speech at the Council on Foreign Relations (September 2010).

58 "Changing Patterns in the Use of the Veto in the Security Council," no date; at: <http://www.globalpolicy.org/images/ pdfs/Changing_Patterns_in_the_Use_of_the_Veto_as_of _August_2012.pdf> (accessed October 3, 2013).

59 Mike Callaghan, "Is the US Holding Back IMF Reform?," *The Lowy Interpreter* (March 18, 2013); at: <http:// www.lowyinterpreter.org/post/2013/03/18/US-leadership -of-the-IMF-under-threat.aspx>.

60 Ruggie, "Multilateralism: The Anatomy of an Institution," p. 8.

61 Ibid., p. 9.
62 Ibid., p. 51.
63 Ibid., p. 56.
64 Ibid., p. 51.
65 Ibid., p. 53.
66 Amitav Acharya, *Whose Ideas Matter?: Agency and Power in Asian Regionalism* (Cornell University Press, 2009).
67 James F. Keeley, "Toward a Foucauldian Analysis of Regimes," *International Organization*, 44/1 (winter 1990): 90.
68 Robert Cox, "The Crisis of World Order and the Problem of International Organization," *International Journal*, 35/2 (1980): 377.
69 In the introductory chapter entitled "Theory of World Politics" in his 1989 book *International Institutions and State Power*, Robert Keohane confessed that: "An unfortunate limitation of this chapter is that its scope is restricted to work published in English, principally in the United States. I recognize that this reflects the Americanocentrism of scholarship in the United States, and I regret it. But I am not sufficiently well-read in works published elsewhere to comment intelligently on them." Robert Keohane, "Theory of World Politics: Structural Realism and Beyond," in Robert O. Keohane, ed., *International Institutions and State Power: Essays in International Relations Theory* (Westview Press, 1989), p. 67 n.1.
70 Robert Cox, "Multilateralism and World Order," *Review of International Studies*, 18/2 (April 1992): 161–80.
71 Francis Wilcox, "Regionalism and the United Nations," *International Organization*, 19 (1965): 789–811. This tendency is more common now in the literature of international political economy than in security. See Jagdish Bhagwati, "Regionalism versus Multilateralism," *The World Economy*, 15/5 (1992): 535–56.
72 Ruggie, "Multilateralism: The Anatomy of an Institution," pp. 3, 4. Ikenberry offers no real explanation for this puzzle, except to say that the US preferred bilateralism and did not see the need for binding institution as attractive to lock in its preponderance because it was so much more hegemonic in Asia than in Europe. He also draws upon Victor Cha's work, which cites fears of entrapment and collusion as the

reasons why the US did not pursue multilateralism in Asia. Ikenberry, *Liberal Leviathan*, p. 101. Ikenberry completely ignores the role of regional norms and the preferences of the large developing countries of Asia, such as India and Indonesia, which opposed US-backed multilateralism, a further testimony to the one-sidedness of the AWO.

73 Donald Crone, "Does Hegemony Matter? The Reorganization of the Pacific Political Economy," *World Politics*, 45/4 (1993): 501–25.
74 Christopher Hemmer and Peter J. Katzenstein, "Why Is There No NATO in Asia? Collective Identity, Regionalism, and the Origins of Multilateralism," *International Organization*, 56/3 (2002): 588.
75 Acharya, *Whose Ideas Matter?*
76 Cox, "Multilateralism and World Order"; Cox, ed., *The New Realism: Perspectives on Multilateralism and World Order* (St Martin's Press, 1997); Michael G. Schechter, ed., *Future Multilateralism: The Political and Social Framework* (Palgrave Macmillan, 1999).
77 Robert O'Brien et al., *Contesting Global Governance: Multilateral Economic Institutions and Global Social Movements* (Cambridge University Press, 2000).
78 James Ron, "Legitimate or Alien? Human Rights Organizations in the Developing World," paper circulated at the Workshops on Religion and Human Rights Pragmatism: Promoting Rights across Cultures, Columbia University New York, September 24, 2011.
79 Ibid.
80 Ibid.

Chapter 4   Emerging Powers: The Hype of the Rest?

1 Andrew F. Cooper, "Labels Matter: Interpreting Rising Powers through Acronyms," in Alan S. Alexandroff and Andrew F. Cooper, eds, *Rising States, Rising Institutions* (The Center for International Governance Innovation and Brookings Institutions, 2010), p. 76.
2 *The EUISS 2030 Report*, p. 118.
3 Jim O'Neill, "Building Better Global Economic BRICS," *Global Economics Paper*, 66 (Goldman Sachs, November

30, 2001). Available at: <http://www.goldmansachs.com /our-thinking/topics/brics/brics-reports-pdfs/build-better -brics.pdf> (accessed December 21, 2012). Although primarily economic in focus, the report did argue giving the BRICs a greater role in global institutions.

4 "Is This the 'BRICs Decade'?," *BRICS Monthly*, 10/3 (Goldman Sachs) (May 20, 2010); available at: <http://www. goldmansachs.com/our-thinking/topics/brics/brics-reports -pdfs/brics-decade-pdf.pdf> (accessed December 21, 2012).

5 Sharma, *Breakout Nations*.

6 G-20 members include: Argentina, Australia, Brazil, Canada, China, European Union, France, Germany, India, Indonesia, Italy, Japan, Mexico, Russia, Saudi Arabia, South Africa, South Korea, Turkey, United Kingdom, United States.

7 Cited in Michael A. Glosny, "China and the BRICs: A Real (but Limited) Partnership in a Unipolar World," available at: <http://guaciara.files.wordpress.com/2010/05/glosny _2009.pdf> (accessed June 7, 2013).

8 A recent initiative is the so-called BRICS Bank, announced at the Durban Summit in 2013. But some see it as a "measure of desperation," which is "still a long way from becoming a reality"; at: <http://newindianexpress.com /editorials/Reform-the-IMF-to-avert-needless-competition /2013/04/20/article1552634.ece>.

9 Amar Bhattacharya, "Enhancing the G20's Inclusion and Outreach," in "Shaping the G-20 Agenda in Asia: The 2010 Seoul Summit," *East–West Dialogue*, 5 (April 2010): 5; available at: <http://www.eastwestcenter.org/fileadmin /stored/pdfs/dialogue005.pdf> (accessed July 7, 2013).

10 Cited in "Recovery or Relapse: The Role of the G-20 in the Global Economy"; available at: <http://www.brookings. edu/~/media/Research/Files/Reports/2010/6/18%20g20%20 summit/0618_g20_summit.pdf> (Washington, DC, June 2010) (accessed December 21, 2012).

11 Javier Solana, "The Cracks in the G-20," Project Syndicate, September 8, 2010; available at: <http://www.project-syndicate. org/commentary/the-cracks-in-the-g-20> (accessed December 21, 2012).

12 David Shorr and Thomas Wright, "The G20 and Global Governance: An Exchange," *Survival*, 52/2 (April–May 2010): 181.

13 Bruce Jones, "Making Multilateralism Work: How the G-20 Can Help the United Nations," Policy Analysis Brief, Muscatine, Iowa: The Stanley Foundation, April 2010.

14 "G-20 Ministers Agree 'Historic' Reforms in IMF Governance"; at: <http://www.imf.org/external/pubs/ft/survey/so/2010/new102310a.htm> (accessed December 21, 2012).

15 See: <http://www.globalpolicy.org/component/content/article/185/41128.html>.

16 Jean-Pierre Lehmann, comment, distributed by email by CUTS-TradeForum; see: <cutscitee@gmail.com> (May 10, 2013).

17 Mahani Zainal Abidin, "The G20: Just Another Annual Get-Together of Leaders?," in "Shaping the G-20 Agenda in Asia," p. 8.

18 Solana, "The Cracks in the G-20."

19 Amar Bhattacharya, "Embracing the G20's Inclusion," in "Shaping the G-20 Agenda in Asia," p. 6.

20 Andrew F. Cooper, "The G20 as the Global Focus Group: Beyond the Crisis Committee/Steering Committee Framework" (G20 Information Centre, Munk School of Global Affairs, University of Toronto, June 29, 2012).

21 Tan See Seng and Amitav Acharya, eds, *Bandung Revisited: The Legacy of the 1955 Asian-African Conference for International Order* (Singapore University Press, 2008).

22 James B. Quilligan, "G20 Leaders to Global South: 'Stimulate This!' at: <http://www.stwr.org/global-financial-crisis/g20-leaders-to-global-south-stimulate-this.html> (London: Share The World's Resources, July 1, 2009)."

23 *New Directions in Brazilian International Relations* (Woodrow Wilson International Center for Scholars, 2007), p. 4; at: <http://www.wilsoncenter.org/topics/pubs/english.brazil.foreignpolicy.pdf> (accessed October 3, 2013).

24 Acharya, "How Ideas Spread: Whose Norms Matter?"; Amitav Acharya, *Whose Ideas Matter?*; Amitav Acharya, "Norm Subsidiarity and Regional Orders."

25 Marc Williams, "Re-articulating the Third World Coalition: The Role of the Environmental Agenda," *Third World Quarterly*, 14/1 (1993): 20–1. See also Mitsuru Yamamoto, "Redefining the North–South Problem," *Japan Review of International Affairs*, 7/2 (fall 1993): 263–81.

26 Acharya and Johnston, *Crafting Cooperation*.
27 Cooper, "Labels Matter."
28 Andrew Hurrell, "Brazil: What Kind of Rising State," in Alexandroff and Cooper, *Rising States, Rising Institutions*, p. 140.
29 *NIC 2030 Report*; *EUISS 2030 Report*.
30 Hurrell, "Brazil: What Kind of Rising State," p. 140.
31 Yan, "New Values for New International Norms," pp. 22–3. It should be stressed that some of these principles proposed by Yan are illustrated with explicit reference to the statements of Chinese leaders, and hence appear geared toward justifying China's domestic and external policies.
32 Ramesh Thakur and Thomas G. Weiss, "R2P: From Idea to Norm – and Action?," *Global Responsibility to Protect*, 1/1 (2009): 22–53.
33 Amitai Etzioni, "Sovereignty as Responsibility," *Orbis*, 50/1 (winter 2006): 71.
34 All quotes taken from Adekeye Adebajo and Chris Landsberg, "The Heirs of Nkrumah: Africa's New Interventionists," *Pugwash Occasional Papers*, 2/1 (January 2001); at: <http://www.pugwash.org/reports/rc/como_africa.htm>.
35 Mohamed Sahnoun, "Uphold Continent's Contribution to Human Rights," July 21, 2009; available at: <http://allafrica.com/stories/200907210549.html?viewall=1> (accessed May 3, 2013).
36 See: <http://www.responsibilitytoprotect.org/files/R2Pcs%20Frequently%20Asked%20Question.pdf>.

Chapter 5   Regional Worlds

1 Winston Churchill, *The Second World War*, vol. 4 (The Reprint Society, 1953), p. 646.
2 Acharya and Johnston, *Crafting Cooperation*.
3 "About the Program," at: <http://regionalworlds.uchicago.edu/about.html> (accessed December 27, 2012); "Area Studies, Regional Worlds: A White Paper for the Ford Foundation," The Globalization Project, University of Chicago, p. 23; available at: <http://regionalworlds.uchicago.edu/areastudiesregworlds.pdf> (accessed December 27, 2012).
4 Sita Ranchod-Nilsson, "Regional Worlds: Transforming Pedagogy in Area Studies and International Studies," p. 8;

at: <http://regionalworlds.uchicago.edu/transformingpeda gogy.pdf> (accessed December 26, 2012).

5 Arjun Appadurai, in "The Future of Asian Studies," *Viewpoints* (Association of Asian Studies, 1997), p. 6.

6 Bjorn Hettne and Andras Inotai, *The New Regionalism: Implications for Global Development and International Security* (UNU World Institute for Development Economics Research, 1994). In this report, which is the foundational document of the new regionalism approach, the distinction between "hegemonic" and "autonomous" regionalism, a crucial aspect of new regionalism, was taken from this author's earlier work: Acharya, "Regional Military-Security Cooperation in the Third World: A Conceptual Analysis of the Relevance and Limitations of ASEAN," *Journal of Peace Research*, 29/1 (1992): 7–21. For subsequent development of new regionalism approach, see Björn Hettne, András Inotai and Osvaldo Sunkel, *Globalism and the New Regionalism* (Palgrave Macmillan, 1999). See also Mario Telò, *European Union and New Regionalism: Regional Actors and Global Governance in a Post-Hegemonic Era* (Ashgate, 2007).

7 Bjorn Hettne and Andras Inotai, *The New Regionalism: Implications for Global Development and International Security.*

8 Amitav Acharya, "The Emerging Regional Architecture of World Politics" (Review Essay), *World Politics*, 59/4 (July 2007): 630.

9 Acharya and Johnston, *Crafting Cooperation.*

10 Peter J. Katzenstein, *A World of Regions: Asia and Europe in the American Imperium* (Cornell University Press, 2005).

11 Hemmer and Katzenstein, "Why Is There No NATO in Asia?".

12 Acharya, "Lessons of Bandung, Then and Now"; Acharya, *Whose Ideas Matter?*.

13 Amitav Acharya, "Competing Communities: What the Australian and Japanese Ideas Mean for Asia's Regional Architecture," *PacNet*, 70 (October 27, 2009); at: <http://csis.org /files/publication/pac0970.pdf>.

14 *EUICSS 2030 Report*, p. 125.

15 *NIC 2030 Report.*

16 Clinton, "The New American Moment."

17 Joseph S. Nye, *Peace in Parts: Integration and Conflict in Regional Organization* (University Press of America, 1987).

18 Amitav Acharya, "Regionalism: The Meso Public Domain in Latin America and South-East Asia," in Daniel Drache, ed., *The Market or the Public Domain: Global Governance and the Asymmetry of Power* (Routledge, 2001), pp. 296–318.

19 For a more detailed discussion, see Amitav Acharya, "Regionalism and the Emerging World Order: Sovereignty, Autonomy, Identity," in Shaun Breslin, Christopher W. Hughes, Nicola Phillips, and Ben Rosamond, eds, *New Regionalisms in the Global Political Economy* (Routledge, 2002), pp. 20–32.

20 Jürgen Ruland, Heiner Hanggi, and Ralf Roloff, eds, *Inter-regionalism and International Relations* (Routledge, 2006).

21 Ian Bremmer, "Decline of Global Institutions Means We Best Embrace Regionalism," FT.Com (January 27, 2012); at: <http://blogs.ft.com/the-a-list/2012/01/27/decline-of-global-institutions-means-we-best-embrace-regionalism/>.

22 Marc L. Busch and Helen V. Milner, "The Future of the International Trading System: International Firms, Regionalism, and Domestic Politics," in Richard Stubbs and Geoffrey R. D. Underhill, *Political Economy and the Changing Global Order* (St Martin's Press, 1994), pp. 259–76.

23 World Trade Organization, "Regionalism: Friends or Rivals?"; at: <http://www.wto.org/english/thewto_e/whatis_e/tif_e/bey1_e.htm> (accessed June 16, 2013).

24 Acharya, *Whose Ideas Matter?*.

25 Ross Garnaut, *Open Regionalism and Trade Liberalization* (Institute of Southeast Asian Studies and Allen and Unwin, 1996), p. 6.

26 Tom Moylan, "Is Regionalism a Threat to Trade Liberalization?," April 10, 2013; at: <http://www.e-ir.info/2013/04/10/is-regionalism-a-threat-to-trade-liberalization/>.

27 World Trade Organization, "Regionalism: Friends or Rivals?"

28 "Regionalism and the Multilateral Trading System: The Role of Regional Trading Arrangements," OECD Policy Brief, August 2003; available at: <http://www.oecd.org/trade/benefitlib/8895922.pdf>; Moylan, "Is Regionalism a Threat to Trade Liberalization?"

29 Pascal Lamy, "Stepping Stones or Stumbling Blocks? The EU's Approach Towards the Problem of Multilateralism vs

Regionalism in Trade Policy," *The World Economy*, 25/10 (2002): 1399–1413.

30 Shaun Breslin, Richard Higgott, and Ben Rosamond, "Regions in Comparative Perspective," in Breslin et al., *New Regionalisms in the Global Political Economy*, p.13.

31 *Regionalization* is different from *regionalism*. The former refers to the emergence of transnational production structures within a given geographic area. In East Asia, regionalization has been defined as a form of "market-driven" regionalism in which the state only plays a facilitating role. Regionalism is a more political concept; it may or may not have a material basis in transnational production.

32 Acharya, *Whose Ideas Matter?*.

33 Katzenstein, *A World of Regions*.

34 Acharya and Johnston, *Crafting Cooperation*. See especially the chapters on Africa, Asia, and Latin America, as well as the conclusion that calls for judging regional institutions in terms of their set goals or foundational objectives.

35 Acharya, "How Ideas Spread: Whose Norms Matter?"

36 George F. Kennan, "A Fateful Error," *New York Times*, February 5, 1997.

37 Robert Kagan, *Power and Weakness, Policy Review*, 113 (June/July 2002); at: <http://www.hoover.org/publications/policy-review/article/7107>.

38 John J. Mearsheimer, *The Tragedy of Great Power Politics* (W. W. Norton & Company, 2001), p. 402.

39 John J. Mearsheimer, "China's Unpeaceful Rise," *Current History* (April 2006): 160–2.

40 Amitav Acharya, "Beyond the Chinese Monroe Doctrine," *Straits Times* (Singapore) (June 20, 2011).

41 Acharya, "Will Asia's Past Be Its Future?".

42 Weber and Jentleson, *The End of Arrogance*.

Chapter 6   Worlds in Collusion

1 Zakaria, *The Post-American World*, p. 242.

2 Katzenstein, *A World of Regions*.

3 Here I draw upon my ideas of "consociational security order" (CSO). CSO and its application to Asian security order is articulated in Amitav Acharya, "Power Shift or Paradigm Shift: China's Rise and Asia's Security Orders," *International Studies Quarterly* (2013).

4 Zbigniew Brzezinski, "After America," *Foreign Policy* (January–February 2012); at: <http://www.foreignpolicy.com/articles/2012/01/03/after_america>.
5 Ikenberry, *Liberal Leviathan*, p. 310.
6 Zakaria, *The Post-American World*. As *The Economist* magazine noted in reviewing Zakaria's book, "Of the roughly three dozen or so contemporary thinkers whose ideas the author praises in the text and uses to make sense of it all, most are not just in America, but based in the north-east corridor that links Boston, New York and Washington, DC." "The Rise of the Rest," *The Economist* (May 22, 2008).
7 Weber and Jentleson, *The End of Arrogance*.
8 Thomas L. Friedman and Michael Mandelbaum, *That Used To Be Us* (Farrar, Straus and Giroux, 2011).

Index